TROLLEYBUSES IN LONDON'S DOCKLANDS

Between Silvertown and North Woolwich the overhead was supported almost entirely by single bow-string bracket arms which were sited on the north side of Albert Road – this was due to the proximity of a railway which precluded conventional means of support. However, it was necessary to position an overhead feeder adjacent to the 'Henley Arms' where a pair of traction poles was installed. The footbridge on the left allows pedestrians to cross the railway line to North Woolwich. On 29th September 1959 E1 582 on route 669 to North Woolwich passes through Silvertown. (John Clarke)

Adam Gordon Books

The dockland areas of London generated a lot of employment with the Royal Victoria Dock and Royal Albert Dock being served by trams and trolleybuses for many years; it cannot be underestimated how important a part they played in the East End during war and peace. Seen at the Victoria and Albert Docks terminus of trunk routes 687/697/699 are J3 974 and K1 1058 which are new to the scene in comparison to E2 607 which spent virtually its whole career on these routes. (John Wills)

Front cover. Route 669 worked between North Woolwich and Stratford Broadway. Operating on this service in October 1959 is E2 607 which has recently arrived at North Woolwich; the driver will put 607 on full lock and park up on the other side of the road ready to take on passengers for its next trip to Stratford Broadway. (Tony Packer)

Rear cover. Route 685 was projected beyond Canning Town to Victoria Docks, Silvertown Station and even North Woolwich to accommodate dockers' shifts. Approaching Silvertown is L3 1398. (Phil Tatt, courtesy Online Transport Archive)

ISBN 978-1-910654-05-7
Publication no. 109
Published in 2015 by Adam Gordon, Kintradwell Farm House, Brora, Sutherland KW9 6LU.
Tel: 01408 622660
E-mail: adam@ahg-books.com

Designed, Typeset & Printed by Henry Ling Limited, at the Dorset Press, Dorchester DT1 1HD

INTRODUCTION

On 6th June 1937, trolleybus services were introduced to the dockland areas of London; four routes started that day. The 669 operated between Stratford Broadway and Canning Town with the others working between Victoria and Albert Docks and Chingford Mount. The 687 travelled via Custom House, Forest Gate and Hoe Street with the 697 passing through Custom House, Stratford and Hoe Street; the 699's line of route was via Prince Regent Lane, Stratford and Hoe Street. The next service to be introduced was the 689 which occurred on 12th September 1937. It worked between Stratford Broadway and East Ham Town Hall; between Upton Park and East Ham it operated in clockwise and anti-clockwise directions; soon afterwards the anti-clockwise service was numbered 690. Route 685 had been inaugurated in January 1937 operating between Walthamstow Crooked Billet and Lea Bridge Road; on 12th September 1937 it was extended to Canning Town. On the same day the 669 was projected to North Woolwich. Route 685 was extended on 4th August 1938 to Royal Victoria Docks, on 24th May 1939 to Silvertown and on 8th May 1940 some journeys reached North Woolwich. On 5th February 1939, route 647 commenced, operating between Stamford Hill and London Docks. On 11th June 1939 the 687 was curtailed at Leyton Depot though on 29th July 1942 it was diverted in Leyton and travelled via Church Road and Markhouse Road to the 'Crooked Billet' at Walthamstow.

London Transport's final changeover from trams to trolleybuses occurred on 9th June 1940 when routes 567 and 665 commenced.

The 567 worked between Aldgate and East Ham Town Hall with some Saturday afternoon journeys to Barking; Smithfield was its inner terminus on Sundays. The 567 had reached Barking daily by 1942 and in April 1949 was serving served Smithfield daily. Route 665 operated daily between Barking and Bloomsbury. 10th June 1940 saw the introduction of weekday peak hour service 565 which worked between Holborn Circus and East Ham Town Hall; it was projected to Barking on 23rd July 1941. The Second World War saw a heavy increase in loadings and London Transport rose to this. On 23rd July 1941 route 569 was introduced and operated in weekday peak hours between Aldgate and Silvertown; on 29th October 1941 it was extended to North Woolwich. Passenger loadings declined in the first half of the 1950s and the 565 was deemed surplus to requirements – it last operated on 16th October 1956.

The dockland areas of London featured in stages four, five, six and eleven of the trolleybus to bus changeover. Routes 567, 569 and 665 were withdrawn after operation on 10th November 1959. Following in their footsteps were the 669, 685, 689 and 690 which ran for the last time on 2nd February 1960. Routes 687, 697 and 699 ceased to operate on 26th April 1960; these east London services closed with due ceremony that night leaving the 647 as the sole route to serve London's Docklands. This service concluded on 18th July 1961.

575C takes on passengers in Canning Town while heading for CROOKED BILLET on the 685; it is believed that the destination display shown was the only one that incorporated three via points. Nissen huts, evocative of the post-war period, can be seen in the background – an RTW on route 15 heads east. (Alan Cross)

Photographed within a few minutes of each other at Stratford on 15th June 1938, E2 622 and D2 416 from West Ham depot are both working on the short but busy 689 circular service. Seen turning out of Tramway Avenue into the Broadway, 622 was the famous 'Daisy Parsons' trolleybus which inaugurated services from West Ham in June 1937 and is still in original condition including the silver roof now much discoloured with dirt. Looking far smarter, having been quite recently overhauled and converted from half to full-cab internal layout, 416 now sports an all-over gloss-painted red roof. 416 is still less than two years old and is already at its third operating base, having previously worked from Hanwell and Hammersmith before arriving at West Ham. No. 622 is an AEC and 416 a Leyland, West Ham being one of the few depots to have permanently mixed allocations of both makes, a situation which persisted at West Ham until June 1954. D2 416 moved to Bexleyheath depot during the war where it remained until withdrawal in March 1959. (London Transport Museum U27357/27358)

To enable 689s/690s to keep to schedule on 'tight' running time higher-powered vehicles were normally used after 1940. It was unusual, therefore, to find E2 613 at Stratford on route 689 in May 1959. Maybe a vehicle had failed and with no J, L, M or N class handy in West Ham depot, 613 was pressed into service. There were no short-working points on these routes so if late running occurred, a whole journey was lost.

The cobbled stand outside St John's church at Stratford was used principally by routes 669/689/690; usually no other service used it so 1401 on the 699 must have been running very late to turn here. It is only going to West Ham depot and the crew may have had it in their minds that if they could go straightaway they could finish early – the presence of an inspector prevents this! The chalked '163' is a 669 running number – it must have been on that route recently. 1401's driver reads a newspaper while his conductor chats to a colleague; it is a hot day as 1401's windscreens and top deck windows are open. At its first loading point, in Tramway Avenue, 1401 will be on the wrong set of wires for a 699; this will be corrected once it has passed through the trailing frog there. (John Wills)

L3 1400 is receiving attention from the West Ham breakdown wagon crew; 1400 has suffered a dewirement (probably on one of the Stratford frogs) and the trolleys are being straightened. It is the last Sunday of operation of route 669 (31st January 1960) and some West Ham drivers are giving their breakdown staff a hard time that weekend – see photo on page 102. (Jack Gready)

Pole 26 at Stratford Broadway held the frog pull handle for 697s/699s to turn left into Tramway Avenue. The canvas hut is shelter for a light duty man pulling the handle; also attached to the pole is a light switch for street lighting purposes. Passing by in the last days of route 208A (May 1959) is RF484 whose radiator flap is untidily in the 'down' position. RF 461 heads back to Dalston garage; at Hackney it will turn off line of route and travel a long way in 'when working' mode – 'when working' meant running in service back to the home garage. The fare chart allowed passengers to travel from Maryland Station to Dalston Garage (and vice versa) – not that anybody ever did. (Alfred Monk, courtesy Roger Monk)

The earlier classes needed their front destination blinds to be changed by the conductor; the E1s came into this category and 597's housing at the front of the top deck has been pulled back for this purpose. The conductor is about to change the 669 display from STRATFORD BROADWAY to NORTH WOOLWICH VIA CANNING TOWN. Passing by is RLH 56 on route 178, the double-deck replacement for RF operated 208A. (John Wills)

A miserable day at Stratford finds 1445 on the 690 and 1521 on the 689 on the time-honoured stand. Running wires and an electrical feeder for withdrawn routes 661 and 663 have been removed – to avoid disturbing span arrangements, hangers remain in place. (Dave Berwick)

Trolleybuses on the 690 waited time outside St John's Church; in this instance 1546 has by-passed the stand and uses the 697/699 wires on 29th October 1955. It is assumed that 1546 has run out of West Ham depot to pick up service here and has not used the stand because other vehicles are parked on it – 1654 on route 669, with untidily set blinds, is one. (David Clarke)

Stratford Broadway looking west in the first part of 1937 with wiring already in place for the first stage of the trolley-bus conversion scheme in the area scheduled for 6th June. Trams terminating at Stratford from the south operate in both directions through the aptly named Tramway Avenue (on the left of the photograph) to stand in the Broadway. Trolleybuses looped from Tramway Avenue to return southwards via West Ham Lane – this wiring can be clearly seen; note the temporary trailing frog which will be removed once trams on routes 1/1A are withdrawn in September. Typical vehicles serving the heavy passenger traffic along the main road into London are a nearly-new STL bus on the 25B and a former Leyton Council E3 tram on route 61. (Charles Topham)

Ex West Ham and now London Transport trams 289 and 242 on routes 99 and 69 respectively stand outside Stratford church on 5th April 1937. Work is well in progress for trolleybuses to show their faces two months later – this will be the commencement of routes 669/697/699 on 6th June. At the moment just a single track of trolleybus overhead is strung; no additional wires will be erected in this part of Stratford until the approach of the 661/663 services which start on 5th November 1939. (Alfred Monk, courtesy Roger Monk)

At the top of Tramway Avenue, former West Ham Corporation tram and now London Transport 276, prepares to turn right into The Broadway in the final days of its operating career. To the right, a former LCC M1 class car can just be glimpsed turning into Tramway Avenue while an E3 on tram route 61 passes by on the main road. Trolleybus wires are in situ with 276 using the positive one.

Seen at the same place as the previous view but over twenty years later, 1382 is only going to Victoria Docks; it is the summer of 1959, the time when 'The Boy and the Bridge' film was advertised. 1382 moved from West Ham to Highgate depot in April 1960 but was one of a few L3s not forwarded later to Fulwell – it ended up in Colindale scrapyard in April 1961.

Walthamstow operated some C1s between 1952 and 1955; one was 153 which has recently been repainted; it retains its offside (though now disused) conductor's sliding signalling window. C1s transferred from Fulwell and Isleworth to Highgate had their sidelights repositioned and placed at the side of the cab. Those going to Walthamstow did not undergo this modification and 153 retained its 'police lights' above the windscreen until withdrawal. It is without front adverts in Tramway Avenue while working on route 699. (Martin Brown)

Six trolleybuses were delivered with sliding ventilator windows rather than half-drops. 1470/1471/1472/1527/1528 had five on each side of the top deck and three on each side of the lower deck; 1529 only had two in each deck on both sides – wartime damage or was it always like this? The driver gives a hand signal to indicate that he is pulling away from a stop in Tramway Avenue. (Ron Wellings)

E2 615 is carrying out a most mysterious movement. Seen in Tramway Avenue on route 697, it is only going to Plaistow Station which was wired for vehicles turning from the south; it will therefore have to use the loop in the wrong direction. When 615 gets to Plaistow, it will use its traction batteries to access Bull Road and use the overhead before 'batterying' out from Holbrook Road to regain the northbound overhead – it will be 'poles down' and 'poles up' at Plaistow. (Ron Wellings)

1666 is in Tramway Avenue, having just passed the facing frog that leads into West Ham Lane; this allowed vehicles to turn short at Stratford from the east and the north. The overhead layout allows passengers on routes 669/689/690 to board separately from those on the 697/699; in the background, the bridling for the short-working curve gives rise to an odd looking arrangement of hangers at the trailing frog. Occasionally 695s were curtailed at Stratford Broadway, giving rise to SAs being seen in Tramway Avenue; one day, an SA was making the U-turn into West Ham Lane when the driving seat collapsed under Driver Baird – it was only by good fortune that no injury was sustained. To Mr Baird, it seemed that the road had collapsed but he, his conductor and an inspector propped the seat up temporarily, enabling the vehicle to limp back to Ilford depot. (Robert Jowitt)

West Ham Lane in late pre-war days and 653 (the highest numbered E3) heads for East Ham Town Hall in the days before a 'lazy' display was introduced on the 689/690 circulars. Southbound operation on this short stretch of West Ham Lane ceased, it is thought, on 10th November 1947. The loop from Tramway Avenue into West Ham Lane is seen on the upper left. West Ham Lane is used in both directions at this time. (Charles Klapper)

West Ham Lane in the mid-1950s finds E1 588 heading for Stratford Broadway stand; the conductor has already turned the blind for its next journey to North Woolwich on the 669. No front advertisements are fitted to 588. (Ron Wellings)

Route 689 was introduced on 12th September 1937, working both ways around the East Ham loop. The public was immediately confused by this and the anti-clockwise service was re-numbered 690. Although there is an entry in the London Transport allocation books for trams and trolleybuses for 28th October 1937, this was purely a schedule change. Just over 80 trolleybuses needed new route blinds, route plates and farecharts – all this takes time and the changes occurred on 14th December 1937. As an aside, the same occurred to the 543 service which was introduced in February 1939 with the clockwise section of the Holborn loop not being re-numbered 643 until April 1939.

697
HIGH ROAD LEYTON
STRATFORD BDY
PLAISTOW STN
BALAAM STREET
FREEMASONS RD
CUSTOM HOUSE
697

Two forms of electric transport one new and one old in West Ham Lane during the three month period (June to September 1937) that the two worked together in this street. Trolleybuses operate on the services to the Victoria and Albert Docks and soon will replace the East Ham circulars. A veritable ex-West Ham Corporation four-wheeler follows an E3 trolleybus southbound on route 697 while a D2 on the 699 is just a few minutes away from Stratford.

E2 607 is at the Church Street North/Church Street junction; it shows the wrong destination for the 669 – the conductor has changed the blind prematurely. From Church Street North, the positive and negative wires take slightly different paths between the crossing and the trailing frog. (Brian Speller)

In 1954 an exchange of vehicles between West Ham and Walthamstow depots saw some J2s operating out of West Ham. One was 977 which, on 15th August 1959, has just passed under a bowstring bracket arm and about to move under span wire construction in Church Street. To the left are the grounds of West Ham parish church. (Clarence Carter)

Prior to the introduction of trolleybuses in Plaistow, this was the vista near Vaughan Place in Church Street. Traction standards were never planted on holy ground and West Ham churchyard is no exception; therefore bowstring traction poles are positioned on one side of the road and support both lines of overhead. The old tram standards (with spiked finials) will soon go for scrap. In the foreground is a facing tramcar crossover; in the far background an ex-London County Council M class tramcar uses the yet-to-be-commissioned trolleybus overhead. (Charles Topham)

More than twenty years after the previous view, the buildings in the vicinity of Vaughan Place have disappeared, probably due to war damage. Although the majority of trolleybuses that used Church Street were AECs, Walthamstow depot had a large number of Leylands; one was K1 1278 which passes the covered entrance to West Ham church on the 697.

This sequence of views illustrates some of the post-war regeneration that took place in the East End in the late 1950s/early 1960s. In Plaistow, which suffered terribly from bombs, Doodlebugs and rocket attacks during the war, new houses and flats were constructed. Plaistow Road was subject to improvement in three main phases, starting in the late summer of 1957 with the widening of the stretch between Bull Road and Holbrook Road (the beginning and end of the Plaistow Station turning circle). This was followed by a more ambitious project, the construction of New Plaistow Road (which formed a Church Street bypass); commencing at the junction of Holbrook Road with Plaistow Road this wide new road was driven through to West Ham Lane, resulting in a significant realignment of the trolleybus route in the process. Finally, early in 1959, the road-makers turned their attention to the section south of Bull Road which was completed in time for trolleybuses on routes 669/697/699 to use until April 1960.

1402 heading south to DOCKS on the 697 is by John Street in Plaistow Road on 23rd April 1960; three other trolleybuses (on the 697 or 699) follow – a regular frequency is not being maintained. In years gone by public baths were a facility provided by local councils. (Peter Mitchell)

On 1st August 1953 E1 574 has pulled up at an old style compulsory bus stop in Plaistow Road at the point where road re-alignment will soon commence; the building of flats and houses is in full swing. 574's nearside advert has seen better days – any Crosse & Blackwell representatives who come across 574 are likely to be in touch with London Transport's advertising department. (Clarence Carter)

Just a short distance further on and around the corner, 1503 waits at a 'dolly' stop (visible through the drivers nearside screen, next to the girl seated on the wall); it stands in the re-aligned part of the carriageway, now re-named New Plaistow Road. The start of the projection of this road through to West Ham Lane can be seen, fenced off, to the left. The flats under construction in the previous view are now occupied.

A woman and two children have just alighted from 1397 at the dolly stop and wait for a motorcycle to pass before crossing the road; a 'Corona' lorry with its cargo of soft drinks is pursued by a van towards Church Street. A fence still bars access to the new roadworks on which workmen are engaged in the background. This view is at the end of Holbrook Road; the exit from the Plaistow Station short-working can be seen. (Don Thompson)

17th May, 1940

The Secretary,
Ministry of Transport,
Metropole Buildings,
Northumberland Avenue,
LONDON, W.C.2.

Our ref: AA2/272
Your ref: PUT.529

Sir,

LONDON PASSENGER TRANSPORT ACT. 1935

TURNING POINT FOR TROLLEY VEHICLES
BULL ROAD, WILLIS ROAD AND
HOLBROOK ROAD, WEST HAM

With reference to your letter of 8th May, I am directed to submit the following observations upon the objections which have been made to the Board's application.

The main purpose of the application is to deal with traffic during the morning and evening peak periods.

During the morning peak there is a large number of workmen at Plaistow Station to be carried to the Docks and other industrial centres in this area, and, as the trolleybuses are usually full by the time they reach this point, vehicles turning short would greatly facilitate the carriage of these workmen, who are engaged on work of national importance.

The situation during the evening peak is further aggravated by the fact that crowds to and from the West Ham Stadium for dog track and speedway events often coincide with workmen on their homeward journey, and, as a very large portion of this traffic only travels as far as Plaistow Station, a turning point in this region would enable the Board to make better provision for these workmen.

The West Ham Corporation have informed the Board that they have no objections to the Board's proposal. As the Corporation are the Education Authority, it is difficult to appreciate the status of the Head Teacher of Holbrook Road School who writes as from the Corporation's Education Department. The only point raised by the Head Teacher is the safety to children using the playground at the school. The Ministry are familiar with this question which has been raised on most of the Board's applications. The Board have shown that by reason of the low rate of speed, the special training of drivers, and the experience of children who live in close proximity to main roads, the apprehensions of objectors are unfounded. As this playground is open from 8 a.m. to 8 p.m., the tendency would be to keep the children from playing in the streets.

With regard to the letter from the Commissioner of Police to the Ministry, the Board note that this proposal is satisfactory from a traffic point of view. With regard to the splaying of the kerb line at the junction of Plaistow Road and Bull Road, the Board, if the application is approved and the Minister so desires, will enter into negotiations with the West Ham Corporation on this point.

The question of the erection of guard rails at the Willis Road entrance to the school is, of course, a matter for the West Ham Corporation.

I return herewith the original petition as requested.

Yours faithfully,

CHIEF LEGAL ADVISER.

Bull Road, Willis Road and Holbrook Road were the streets used by vehicles turning at Plaistow Station. The photographer is standing in Plaistow Road at its junction with Bull Road on 30th January 1960; E2 612 heads for North Woolwich on route 669 while 1542 on the 699 proceeds to Chingford Mount. Right until the end of the 699, trolleybuses used Bull Road circle even on Sunday mornings to accommodate 'dockers'; their shift vagaries were met by efficient scheduling. (John Gillham)

By Bull Road facing frog L3 1432 is running late and has been curtailed at Crooked Billet. A display was not available on West Ham's blinds for this location so the 685 CROOKED BILLET AND LEA BRIDGE RD display suffices. It is 26th April 1960, the last day of route 697 and the 'Stops and Signs' department have yet to move the bus stop flag from a traction pole to a new position. (Tony Belton)

N1 1643 was delivered to Bow depot in November 1939 and remained there for almost twenty years. Arriving at Fulwell works on 26th March 1959 it was released from overhaul on 15th May; a short while in store ensued before it was relicensed on 1st June, being simultaneously transferred to West Ham. Its stay was short as it moved to Stonebridge on 10th November 1959. During its time at West Ham, 1643 turns into Bull Road, working a 'short' on route 669 on 9th July 1959. (John Clarke)

Walthamstow's 1278 is in Bull Road on 26th April 1960 while working on route 699. A pram and tricycle of the time are in view; the people in this panorama are probably oblivious to the fact that electric street traction in the East End is about to conclude. (Fred Ivey)

When working on Plaistow 'shorts', drivers parked in either Willis Road or Holbrook Road. Seen in Willis Road on 23rd January 1960, L3 1447 on the 699 is having a few minutes stand time. Another vehicle is behind – this signals a frequent service to this location in peak hours. (Peter Mitchell)

Some turning points in the East End were in dreary surroundings – this is illustrated by 971 in Willis Road on 26th April 1960. A single traction standard in this street has a bowstring arm. (Fred Ivey)

Standing in Holbrook Road at 12.26pm on Saturday 23rd January 1960 is E2 616 on route 697. 'Shorts' were run to Plaistow Station at this time of the day as 'dockers' work a five and a half day week. (Peter Mitchell)

Leaving Holbrook Road and turning back into Plaistow Road, 1282 is on its way to DOCKS. On this wet day, all the windows are closed – if 1282 takes on a good load of passengers, they will mist up. Football pool advertisements were a good source of revenue for London Transport. (Fred Ivey)

Tuesday 26th April 1960 and 1537 will be transferred to Highgate later that day. 1537 was fitted with a rear offside advertisement during its later days at West Ham; it is assumed that the advert fixer inadvertently positioned a VAT 69 poster on the rear – he had placed two on the front, hence the confusion. This feature would pertain for many months ahead – at Highgate depot. To the very right of the picture, Tony Belton also records the scene near Morley Road in Plaistow Road. Looking south from Bull Road after the completion of roadworks, the miserable weather does little to diminish the beauty of the newly re-aligned overhead wiring, curving gracefully away towards Plaistow station in the distance. Despite being peak hour, Plaistow Road is surprisingly lightly-trafficked. (Fred Ivey)

Poplar and West Ham depots were the last places on the London Transport network where the ticket and punch system was used for fare collection, this occurred on Saturday 4th October 1958, meaning that this view was taken prior to this. The conductor of 1385B pulls the frog handle down outside Plaistow Station; he likes 'travelling light' and keeps coins in his pockets rather than a cash bag – his ticket rack will be in the appropriate slot in the vehicle. When he uses a Gibson machine it will be heavier and 'travelling light' will not be an option. Placing bus stop flags on traction poles meant less street furniture on pavements. (Alan Cross)

The parting of the ways in Plaistow for routes 669/697/699 was originally at the top of Upper Street – it was brought forward four bays in late 1956 to the station with passage of traffic at Upper Street junction being speeded up. This allowed more convenient loading arrangements; two compulsory stops were positioned – one for 697s/699s, the other for 669s. On 30th January 1960, H1 805 is at the most southerly of the two stops, allowing 1390, which has just served its stop, to overtake. 669s had the frog setting in their favour but drivers still had to come off the power to get through the 'dead' section. (Ron Wellings)

Plaistow station was of ornate design; a London Transport bulls-eye surmounts a British Railways totem. On Sunday 21st February 1959 Finlays are closed for the day. 579 heads for DOCKS on route 697. (Allen Smith, courtesy Alan Cross)

Seen at the same place and time but on the opposite side of the road to the previous view, 594 is WH10 on the 697. In the early 1950s some regularly used displays on West Ham's destination blinds were replaced by some motorbus-style ones supplied by Chiswick Bus Works; 594 uses one such panel: CHINGFORD MOUNT CUSTOM HOUSE STRATFORD. (Allen Smith, courtesy Alan Cross).

A close-up of blind displays such as the one illustrated above. The blind is dated 5th October 1949 with an amendment date of 14th October 1953.

Although Walthamstow's C3s were whittled down over the years, a few survived until 1959; working on route 697 the penultimate member of the class, 382, ascends the slope to Plaistow Station. In the background, the original layout, where 669s turn into Upper Road, can just be seen. (Ron Wellings)

Gillham's out again, this time on 30th January 1960, and he photographed a number of East End trolleybus junctions that day. Here he has captured two in one go – Plaistow station and Plaistow Road/Upper Road junction; in the background a K on route 697 waits at a bus stop. (John Gillham)

Approaching Settle Road from Plaistow High Street 1527 (with window 'sliders') heads north on route 699. Drivers were apt to take a seemingly innocuous bend too fast just south of Upper Road, resulting in dewirements; as a precautionary measure, mesh is strung between traction poles to prevent flailing trolley arms causing damage to windows of a local builder's merchant. In spring 1960 an edict was sent to bus garages and trolleybus depots stating that their code should be painted onto the sides of each vehicle; until this time it had been a metal stencil. West Ham still had a large number of trolleybuses at the time but it was not worth painting the code on them as they were about to be transferred or withdrawn. (Fred Ivey)

Colonel E. Woodhouse, on behalf of the Ministry of Transport, inspected trolleybus installations in the Plaistow area on 1st June 1937; the MOT required that a narrow section of a hundred yards in Plaistow High Street be controlled by light signals – white vertical and horizontal arrows. When the system fell into disuse is not known (possibly war damage) but the apparatus did not exist in post-war years. This view of 1406 in the High Street, proceeding south, indicates that two trolleybuses could not safely pass each other here; maybe drivers travelling in opposite directions could see each other and waited until the on-coming vehicle had passed by. But what happened on foggy days? (Michael Dryhurst)

Although the 'Star' newspaper van (advertising the Budget) can easily pass 1283 it is impossible for two trolleybuses to do so – one would have to mount the pavement if they met here in the High Street. When eight foot wide RMs move in, the situation will be exacerbated. It is April 1960 and 1283 has a rosy future as it will be on the streets of London until April 1962; less fortunate is 1533 leaving Clegg Street – it will last run on 26th April. (Fred Ivey)

Trams are still running in Plaistow as an 'ALL CARS STOP HERE' is in place. Maybe some of the strands of wire on the overhead are part of the MOT set-up for trolleybus operation; possibly the box on the tram traction pole, here at Clegg Street, contains signal lights. (Charles Topham)

1470.—NOTICE—SIGNALS, HIGH STREET, PLAISTOW.

The attention of Drivers is drawn to the signals controlling the narrow part of High Street, Plaistow, near Clegg Street.

Signal lights are fixed on—

Pole No. 140	to	Stratford
Pole No. 141	to	Docks

and after passing under the operating skates Drivers must not proceed through the narrow way until they receive the green signal.

No tram or trolleybus must be run under the operating skate or follow another vehicle through until the preceding vehicle has cleared the line.

'PRINCESS ALICE' TO PLAISTOW BROADWAY

At its maximum, the Princess Alice overhead junction was very complex; this was between November 1939 and August 1959. Routes passing through were 663, 685, 687 and 695. No changes took place until the withdrawal of the 663 in August 1959; another alteration occurred when the 685 came off in February 1960. All that was left then were plain wires for the remaining route, the 687. Splices in the overhead, through which 1443 is about to pass on 2nd April 1960, signify alterations. (Ron Wellings)

1501 on route 687 is by Ismailia Road/St George's Road in Upton Lane on 22nd April 1960. In a few days' time she will move away from East London and spend time at Highgate and Fulwell depots where she will finish her days. This means that she will have worked in all parts of London except the south. (Peter Mitchell)

Trams still run past the Spotted Dog public house in Upton Lane (see bottom left). New trolleybus wiring has been erected above the tram wires which will be removed (an overnight job) in time for route 687 to commence on 6th June 1937. Also to go will be the old tram traction pole with its spiked finial – new trolleybus standards will make those in the area redundant. (Charles Topham)

On 6th February 1960 M1 1538 is at the same location as the view above. 'Fairy lights' are positioned between the running wires; when illuminated they assist drivers in ascertaining the correct line to follow in foggy weather. 1538 moved from West Ham to Highgate depot in April 1960; it was withdrawn at the end of January 1961. Nominated for cannibalisation, many of its parts were removed to keep others roadworthy. (Clarence Carter)

L3 1399 passes the 'Spotted Dog' while running into West Ham depot on route 687. This vehicle had a chequered career; originally allocated to West Ham it stayed there until October 1956 when it was transferred to Ilford – it had a two year stay there before returning to West Ham in November 1958. Sent to Highgate at stage six of the conversion programme it was forwarded to Fulwell at the ninth stage. It stayed in service until the last day of trolleybuses in London (8th May 1962) and was not sold to Cohen's until 28th June 1962. Now it is 25th April 1960 and 1399 has only one more day in the East End. Intriguingly, the fairy lights have now been removed – this seemed to be a general practice activated shortly before routes' withdrawal, though nobody seems to know why. (Jack Gready)

Three 687s are at West Ham Park on 9th July 1959. L3s 1390 and 1396 head south while 1516 makes for Crooked Billet. The two gentlemen on either side of Upton Lane wait to cross the road. (John Clarke)

The only trolleybus service to use Upton Lane and Stopford Road was the 687; E1 581 works south on 15th August 1959; passing through the Plashet Road/ Stopford Road crossover. The long coasting arrangement negotiated by the 689/690 circulars and seen on page 116 of 'Trolleybuses in East London' is more clearly illustrated here. (Clarence Carter)

Having just turned out of Stopford Road, 1645 is in the short part of Terrace Road which was traversed by trolleybuses; it is about to turn into Pelly Road on 29th September 1959. Following it 1528 leaves Stopford Road. (John Clarke)

582 is in Clegg Street at its junction with Cromer Street on 21st April 1956; it still sports linen blinds in both front boxes. The housing is of typical East End design. (Peter Mitchell)

967 is coming up to traction pole 376 in Clegg Street. Adjacent to the standard is a large cenotaph feeder pillar from which trunking cables running the length of the traction pole are attached.

The width of a standard London trolleybus is seven feet, six inches; drivers knew the road space they needed and the exact line to be taken at each junction so that trolley arms would not leave the overhead. 1431 turns from Plaistow High Street into Clegg Street. This picture is typical east-end landscape where wartime bomb sites remained undeveloped even into the nineteen-sixties. (Denis Battams)

Apart from the replacement of the original wooden equipment by dumbbell type, the arrangement of the overhead apparatus remains exactly as 23 years previously (see page 24). The turnout has not been brought forward to form a lead-in but remains at the junction; it became common in the late 'fifties to bring turnouts forward at such places, but it is likely that the narrowness of Plaistow High Street and the closeness of the overhead wires would make the addition of a lead-in difficult. 1437 makes the sharp right turn into Clegg Street; although the 687 was less frequent than the combined 697/699 frequency, the 687 had frog priority as it obviated the need for conductors to run into the roadway after their vehicles. There was always an element of danger when this occurred and the conductor will have to watch the van behind 1437 when he/she re-boards. The pulling of frog handles will not be required much longer as 'Buses for Trolleybuses' posters are pasted on traction poles. (Jack Gready)

Seen by Shaftesbury Avenue in Plaistow High Street, 1402 passes beneath one of the bowstring bracket arms used here; the closeness of the two sets of wires is apparent. A boy and his father patronise a vending machine outside the Valletta Café; above is a hoarding for Walls Ice Cream. (Jack Gready)

1542 is at the southern end of Plaistow High Street, about to turn into Balaam Street while working on route 687 to DOCKS. 1542 passed to Highgate depot once West Ham had finished with it in April 1960; it was retired from service twelve months later, at stage ten of the conversion scheme.

Running into West Ham depot on 24th October 1959, N2 1646 is at Plaistow Broadway. It shows WEST HAM GREENGATE ST – a bit odd as WEST HAM DEPOT was nearer the other 699 displays on the blind. (Jack Gready)

699 drivers passing northbound at the Greengate Street/Balaam Street junction had to come off the power pedal to avoid arcing on the overhead. Even though the main stop for 687s/697s that left West Ham depot bound for DOCKS is around the corner in Balaam Street, people can board at the 'white' stop here; wires on the right are for trolleybuses running in and running out of West Ham depot. (John Gillham)

PLAISTOW TO DOCKS VIA PRINCE REGENT LANE

The chassis of service vehicle 740J had previously belonged to motorbus STL 38; it is allocated to the Central Distribution services at Chiswick and is seen at Plaistow Broadway. A bus stop flag is on the back of 740J so maybe its crew are preparing to put a new one up in the vicinity. 1527 works through to DOCKS on route 699. (Fred Ivey)

LONDON PASSENGER TRANSPORT BOARD
(TRAMS AND TROLLEYBUSES)
TIME CARD
CHINGFORD AND DOCKS

TIME SCHEDULE NUMBER **2613**

ROUTES 687, ~~697~~, 699

WEST HAM.

OPERATING ON SATURDAY   LEAVE DEPOT 5.53   RUNNING NUMBER 5H

Ching-ford	Bakers Arms	Thatched House	Wan-stead	Strat-ford	Plaistow Broadway	Abbey Arms	Green Gate	Docks Arrive	Docks Depart	Green Gate	Abbey Arms	Plaistow Broadway	Strat-ford	Wan-stead	Thatched House	Bakers Arms	Ching-ford
							5 55	6 3	6 6	6 14		6 16	6 24		6 30	6 41	6 56
4.3	4 18	4 29		4 35	4 43		4 45	4 53	4 54		8 3						
												8 4 DEPOT					
				11 55	DEPOT												
					11 59		12.8	12 10			12 19	12 22 W. HAM DT.	12 32	12 38	12 49		LEYTON DT. 12 51
LEYTON DT. 12 54	12 58	1 9	1 15		1 25 W. HAM DT.	1 28	1 34	1 39			1 48	1 52					
					1 55	1 59	2 8	2 9			2 18						
												2 22 DEPOT					

NOTE—Both Driver and Conductor are responsible for the vehicle running to the times stated above, and any deviation therefrom will have to be accounted for.

D4/402/73.
(25M-4-38)

It is 24th October 1959 and E2 617 leaves West Ham depot for a trip on route 685 to Victoria Docks (Clyde Road). It is unlikely that any passenger will board 617 in Greengate Street but the farechart allowed passengers to buy a 7d ticket from the depot to Victoria Docks. (Jack Gready)

It is 26th April 1960 and 1392 leaves West Ham depot for the penultimate time; also taking up service is a Routemaster on route 238 which turns right into Greengate Street. Boys on bikes watch movements at the exit – they are clued up to the fact that it is the last day of trolleybuses here. Later that evening 1392 will turn left out of the depot and make its way to Highgate. The thoroughfare next to the depot was intriguingly known as Barbers Alley. (Tony Belton)

1503 carries out a mysterious movement on 30th January 1960 – maybe it has run-in 'light' from Stratford; its next trip would have been to North Woolwich. Two conductresses enter the depot; schoolboys resting their bikes against the depot wall take note of the comings and goings. Within its confines, an RM indicates that West Ham trolleybus depot will soon become West Ham bus garage. (Ron Wellings)

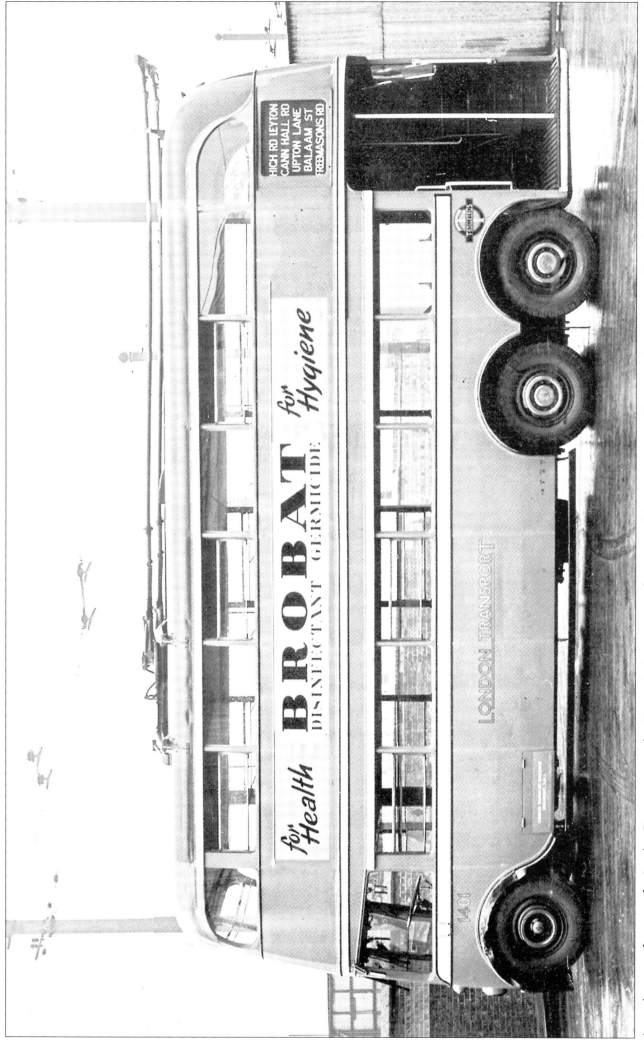

A good source of revenue for London Transport was advertisements; to encourage firms to participate, various vehicles were photographed. West Ham's 1401 is on the depot forecourt on 7th January 1948 advertising Brobat Disinfectant. (London Transport Museum U42004)

HIGH RD LEYTON
CANN HALL RD
UPTON LANE
BALAAM ST
FREEMASONS RD

for Health
BROBAT for Hygiene
DISINFECTANT GERMICIDE

LONDON TRANSPORT

Walthamstow's 1278 has been curtailed in West Ham depot; the driver would have asked someone which road to take inside the building as he would be unfamiliar with its layout. 1278 is ready to go the short distance to Plaistow station but shows the wrong via point as route 699 did not go via Custom House – mind you, this journey did not go via Prince Regent Lane so he's between the devil and the deep blue sea! It is 26th April 1960, the last day that West Ham depot is used for electric traction purposes. (Fred Ivey)

London Transport's war damage log for 19th March 1941 states 'Trolleybus 621 was completely wrecked in Plaistow Road'. It was rebodied by Weymann and renumbered 621A; after spells at Fulwell and Hammersmith depots, it returned to West Ham where it is seen after a stint on the 687. The building on the left is the docking bay; in the background to the right is the substation – both were extensively damaged during the war. (Fred Ivey)

1555 on the left and 1594 on the right are out of service. 1594 has its emergency exit open and may be on loan from Bow to Poplar as it has a Poplar side blind fitted; this has been wound down as far as it can go – it shows part of the display used when EXTRAs were supplied for events at West Ham Stadium. Both vehicles are parked at the entrance to the washing bays. (Fred Ivey)

A number of London United's trolleybuses which passed to London Transport in 1933 were used for training duties once their passenger carrying lives were over. Although its dilapidated appearance on 29th April 1949 implies that A2 58 has been dumped that is not so, for after withdrawal from revenue earning service on 30th September 1948 it took on a training role at West Ham on 21st December 1948 – it continued in this capacity until 31st October 1950. A sticker has been placed over the London Passenger Transport Board legal ownership name after its nationalisation in January 1948; it now belongs to the London Transport Executive. WORKMAN has been wound up on the nearside blind; rather appropriate as wheelbarrows are placed in front of 58 – its rundown condition is exacerbated by its open windows and peeling off advert. Despite this, a notice encourages people to join LTE. (James Aston)

From the mid-fifties, staff shortages were a curse for London Transport; vehicles that should have been carrying passengers were in the depot lying idle for as much as five hours at a time. It would appear that 1498 is a victim of a 'staff cut' at West Ham, and is parked on the forecourt. The former municipal tramways offices and other buildings are receiving attention by the firm responsible for changing the trolleybus depot into a bus garage. A sparkling 1498 brightens the place up. (John Buckle)

622 had been the first trolleybus to leave West Ham depot (6th June 1937); their staff persuaded London Transport that it would be fitting for it to be the last to enter – and it was. It is on the forecourt on 26th April 1960 in the process of being decorated for the last run. A comedian has placed an L plate in 622's windscreen, ready for driver John Hall when he climbs into its cab that night. (Fred Ivey)

A flying bomb hit West Ham depot on 30th July 1944; many vehicles were so badly damaged that rebodying was necessary. One was 1543 which is amongst debris on 8th August. It was many months before West Ham was brought back to full use; it took almost four years for 1543B (as it became) to return to service – even then it went to Holloway depot. (London Transport Museum U35932)

Looking into the forecourt of the southern entrance, folding doors lead into the building which houses service vehicles; one is seen outside one of the customary olive green doors. On the boundary wall, a sign states TROLLEYBUSES. A Mr N. Harrison was commissioned by London Transport to take some photographs of 'progress work' at Clapton, Poplar and West Ham trolleybus depots. This is a premature description as it is 21st August 1957 and work has yet to commence on converting the depot into a bus garage. The wire from the frog handle to the pulley near the top of the traction pole is loose – when the handle is pulled down it will straighten. (London Transport Museum NH/1414)

Having time off in the depot are 1540 and 1535, both unit-constructed M1 class vehicles. 1540 shows WEST HAM GREENGATE STREET, the display used by 689s/690s running into the depot; to have shown WEST HAM DEPOT would have been a long wind through the blind – an aching arm is thus avoided. Alongside with its valance off but still with booms on the overhead, is withdrawn 626C. (John L. Smith)

Arriving at West Ham depot in the early afternoon of 23rd April 1960, M1 1534 may have been out for the Saturday dinner time finish – however, it could be a victim of staff shortage. Out of sight, the conductor is pulling a frog handle which is cantilevered to the depot wall. (Peter Mitchell)

This is the last trip that 1539 will make while working at West Ham depot; the driver opts to enter via the southern entrance – his conductress is about to pull the frog handle down. 1539 has run in from DOCKS on 26th April 1960. On the next day 1539 will be at Highgate depot; another transfer in a year's time will see her at Finchley where she will remain until 7th November 1961. (Tony Belton)

There were two ways for trolley-buses to enter West Ham depot from the south. The more northerly of the two entrances, in the distance, was the one normally used by vehicles coming in; an alternative means was available at the southern entrance. Why go the long way round when the southern frog gives a quicker way in? That's how most of them did it though. This view was taken on 24th October 1959. (John Gillham)

This flimsy Austrian built Cedes Stoll single-decker trolleybus was demonstrated in Greengate Street during September 1912 for the benefit of West Ham Council. It is dwarfed by Corporation tram 114, one of a batch of twelve cars built by Hurst Nelson the previous year. The Cedes Stoll system, which depended on pulling an overhead carriage by cable attached to the roof of the 'trackless' car, found few advocates in Britain.

With West Ham depot/West Ham garage in the background (that is its proper description as it is 21st April 1960 when both modes of transport were in use), 1395 will reach DOCKS in a few minutes time. Soon it will be working from Highgate depot and on many of the routes they operated. (Brian Speller)

There were a few places where, to save expenditure, a three-way wire configuration was installed; they were uni-directional for short distances and near depots. One location was at 'Greengate' West Ham and catered for trolleybuses entering and leaving the nearby depot. A number of trams were retained after the 1937 tram to trolleybus conversions to work specials to West Ham Stadium at the bottom of Prince Regent Lane. One was ex-West Ham 272 which uses the trolleybus trailing frog under the watchful eye of some London Transport employees – maybe 272 is undergoing a test run.

Routes 567 and 699 could only run together between West Ham depot and Greengate Junction. West Ham's 1651 is out of service in Greengate Street while Walthamstow's 889 passes by. (Fred Ivey)

This view looks north-west at Greengate junction on 17th October 1959. The 699 wires go straight ahead while Barking Road routes pass at right-angles. Note the catenary span. The centre wire layout has long gone, but the drawback is that trolleybuses are no longer able to make the west to north movement. (John Gillham)

The centre wire layout was used at Greengate junction for almost three years; one of its frogs is seen in the top middle of the picture. Trams are still running as shown by an E1 taking up service on route 67 to Aldgate; there are no rails for it to turn right from Greengate Street into Barking Road and it has to travel east a short way before it can use a crossover to go west. For this manoeuvre, trams use their own wire – all other movements are via trolleybus overhead. This view was taken between September 1937 and the start of the Second World War as 646 has no war-time blackout markings. (Charles Klapper)

N2 1663 moves from Prince Regent Lane into Greengate Street while working on route 699 on 9th July 1959. With many items of 'special work' aloft, drivers had to know what they were doing with regards to taking power or not here. (John Clarke)

Due to the withdrawal of trolleybuses on Barking Road, all 'special work' has been removed at Greengate junction. On 23rd April 1960 Walthamstow's 1077 waits at traffic lights in Prince Regent Lane; an overhaul late in life saw it pass to Wood Green and Isleworth for further service. At Isleworth 1077 was fitted with the only Charlton-produced blind in the depot; this made it immediately recognisable. In the background, Prince Regent Lane passes over the northern outfall sewer bank – a local landmark in the area! (Jack Gready)

It is 12th March 1960 and M1 1534 surmounts the sewer bank in Prince Regent Lane while working on route 699 to Victoria and Albert Docks. A significant feature in the 'fifties and 'sixties were trees that were pollarded by local councils. (Lyndon Rowe)

E1 586 passes over Beckton Road while working south on 12th March 1959. The frequency of the 699 was very high so it is not surprising that another vehicle (611) has caught it up. (David Clarke)

633C is in Prince Regent Lane approaching its junction with Beckton Road; it is being run out of service into West Ham depot. Rather than travel via Freemasons Road (route 687) the driver returns to the depot using the 699 wires as it is a quicker way home. (Alan Cross)

L3 1453 is outside the Nottingham Arms in Prince Regent Lane on 23rd April 1960. Although a number of trolleybus services in the East End have been withdrawn by now, pedestrians in this street are still only used to seeing trolleybuses which first operated through here on 6th June 1937. (Peter Mitchell)

Routes 697 and 699 used different roads between Plaistow and DOCKS – the 697 via Custom House, the 699 via Prince Regent Lane. H1 798 is at the bottom of Prince Regent Lane about to turn into Connaught Road; E2 607 approaches from Custom House – between them is a moneylender's shop. It was here that, as a young lad, the singer Tommy Steele admitted throwing fireworks onto the platforms of 699s turning from Prince Regent Lane into Connaught Road. (Jack Gready)

Because there was no pavement on the south side of Connaught Road, traction standards were positioned behind a fence and on railway land; one was pole 18 to which was fitted a cantilevered frog handle. The dexterity of the conductor has to be admired as he pulls the handle from 1443's platform while the vehicle moves slowly forward. Practice makes perfect and experience has taught him that there is no need to look up to see whether trolley arms have cleared the points. Conductors were supposed to alight and pull the handle down which no doubt older members of staff did. (Right) 1537 turns right into Prince Regent Lane; the frog setting allows crews an unimpeded run. 1537 again shows the offside rear advert. Both views were taken on 25th April 1960. (Tony Newman)

5.17 p.m. Prince Regent Lane Substation. Both rectifiers tripped out on overload, and some anode fuses blown apparently caused by bus dewirement. Tester arrived at 6.08 p.m. and Substation back on load at 6.18 p.m.

61 mins. passenger delay

Trolleybuses served Victoria and Albert Docks between June 1937 and April 1960 with vehicles being provided by Walthamstow and West Ham depots. The views on the next few pages show the many classes that could be seen there.

It was unusual not to see any trolleybuses parked in Connaught Road on the approach to Docks terminus. However it is a Sunday (24th April 1960) and with a less frequent service being operated; just two are at the loading platform. The request stop flag is superfluous as vehicles tended to have most of their stand time here rather than at the loading area. (John Gillham)

Early in the East End trolleybus era, E1 555 is at the head of a queue of five moving towards the loading bay. 555 (seen on page 49 in original livery) is an EXTRA to Plaistow Broadway which will travel via Prince Regent Lane; the third vehicle is a 687 working to the same location but via Custom House. In between and on the siding is D3 549 on the 687 to Chingford Mount – at the time the siding was accessed by changing booms from the main line to a 'dead-ender'; in 1941 it was 'frogged'-in.

Inspectors required vehicles to depart in the right order here; this was largely achieved by indicating to crews whether to use the siding or not. 1405 and 610 are in their correct positions; the last trolleybus in line is being signalled by the inspector to go onto the siding. (Jack Gready)

The system mentioned previously was not fool-proof as there were times when another vehicle needed to overtake one on the main line. This has happened here and 1534's conductor is dealing with the situation and placing its booms onto the siding; 1527 waits at the rear. 1534's driver has a bit of fun with the photographer while the bamboo pole is repositioned beneath the vehicle. (Geoff Bannister)

Sunday 16th October, 1949.
    6 a.m. Connaught Road Dock Terminus Remote Control wires, corner of Freemasons Road, damaged by scaffolding. Between 6 a.m. and 8 a.m. intermittent delays occurred.

AEC 325 has spats over its rear wheels – Leyland 481, behind, does not. The maintenance staff at Walthamstow preferred 'non-spats' as it could be awkward to remove the 'spats'. Crews at Walthamstow had a wide operating area: Chingford Mount, Winchmore Hill and Woodford in the north, Liverpool Street in the central area and Manor House in between. They also worked in the dockland areas of Silvertown and Custom House. (John L. Smith)

Few photos exist of 1662 – part of its top deck was burnt out in Charlton Works in 1956, resulting in it being scrapped the following year. Before then, it is seen on the siding here. (John L. Smith)

Something has hit 1532 up the back; this occurred shortly before withdrawal so the West Ham coachmakers decided that it was not worth repairing the damage (later on in the conversion programme, some vehicles were withdrawn with far less damage than this). 1532 was an oddity in the fleet in that it had a mixture of sliding and drop-down ventilators in its upper saloon windows – three in the nearside and one in the offside. Maybe war damage saw some of those in 1470 fitted to 1532. (Tony Belton)

Between June 1937 and June 1939, route 687 operated between Victoria and Albert Docks and Chingford Mount via Forest Gate. With few people photographing new trolleybuses at the time, this view of 555 is the best of a 687 showing CHINGFORD MOUNT. There are two items of note on the vehicle in front. 1) Although there is a position for a route plate to be positioned next to the platform, it is not in use – this could be due to the frequent changing of vehicles from one route to another. 2) The side blind abbreviates ROAD and LANE – note the use of a small second letter to them. (Charles Klapper)

Until 1952, C1 138 spent most of its life plodding up and down route 657; the only relief would be bank holiday outings on the 667 to Hampton Court. With the allocation of Q1s into Isleworth that year, 138 became a nomad and spent time at Hammersmith and West Ham depots before moving to Walthamstow on 28th April 1954 (the day London Transport announced the scrapping of the trolleybus system). During its time at Walthamstow, 138 is seen at DOCKS on route 697 and is accompanied by vehicles on the two other routes seen here – 586 on the 687 and an E2 on route 699. The trailing frog is now at the terminus. (Anthony M. Wright, courtesy Gerald Mead)

622 is at DOCKS in the days leading up to April 16th 1960; as previously stated, it was retained in service after stage five of the conversion scheme as the staff wanted it to become the last trolleybus to enter West Ham depot, just as it had been the first to leave in 1937. E2 622 advertises the Used Car Show at Olympia; London Transport's advertising department is at its peak of efficiency for by 26th April when 622 was photographed on the depot forecourt being prepared for its last run (see page 37), 'stock bills' were fitted. It would have done no harm to have left the 'Olympia' adverts on. (Fred Ivey)

Although London Transport considered using a turntable here, conventional means were adopted. This May 1937 view shows trolleybus overhead above tram wiring – it will be adjusted in time for the first 699 to pass through. Trams run a few yards further east than their successors; note their ornate traction poles. A shelter for passengers has yet to be constructed. (London Transport Museum U23880)

By March 1939, a concrete loading shelter and inspector's office surmounted by a flag-post with a bulls-eye had been installed. A queuing system is in force with those wishing to board 687s/697s being segregated from those wanting a 699 – passengers needing a 687/697 board at the rear-most position. White bands surround the traction standards – it is not known why as it is some months before the black-out was implemented. A dockers' shift has just ended and workers are keen to get home; trolleybuses often left here with a full load. To help shift the crowds, D2 424 is an EXTRA 699 on 3rd June 1939. Typifying D2 movements around the system, 424 had originally been at Hanwell depot; upon delivery of F1s there it moved to Hammersmith and later to West Ham. During the war it moved to Bexleyheath where it finished its days. Redundant tram tracks are filled in with tarmac. (London Transport Museum U29899)

Three vehicles are photographed on 3rd June 1939; first in line is a Walthamstow C3 on the 697 going to PLAISTOW BDY; with no turning facility available there it will travel to West Ham depot to turn. The leading trolleybus is in the original livery which incorporated a silver front dome – this was later modified to red as shown by 611 in the rear. (London Transport Museum U29895)

C3 352 is taking on passengers; behind, 364 publicises Ward's Stores of Tottenham who advertised profusely on trolleybuses. With Walthamstow depot operating over a wide area their adverts could be seen at locations far away from their business address; one place was Victoria and Albert Docks – thus the word is spread. 364 was destroyed in West Ham Works during the war; its chassis was used in the construction of 1385B (Charles Klapper)

1379 had a once in a lifetime visit to the Victoria and Albert Docks; this was in May 1954 when the Southern Counties Touring Society hired the vehicle. One of the participants has arranged for '639 KINGS CROSS' to be displayed.

Walthamstow and West Ham depots both worked 'shorts' between DOCKS and Plaistow Station. The Walthamstow blinds incorporated a via point for these trips as seen on a well turned-out 1058; although regular passengers were aware of which roads 697s and 699s used between here and Plaistow, it assisted those unfamiliar with the area. 1058 would remain in service until 8th May 1962. (John Wills)

The initial overhead layout at Connaught Road terminus saw just a circle of wires – this was soon deemed impractical due to the large number of vehicles arriving and departing. Seen on 3rd September 1937, E3 652 waits at the loading point – unusually, no other vehicles are in view. In the background, smoke bellows from an industrial chimney. In the foreground, the recently abandoned tram tracks feature prominently. Horse drawn vehicles were still *de rigeur* for commercial purposes at this time. (London Transport Museum U24723)

Each turning circle had to be constructed individually; in this instance the lack of span wires on the inside of the circle is because it is held aloft purely by the tension in the running wires. 1533 leaves the terminus on 6th February 1960. (Clarence Carter)

This view shows the tram turning arrangements in 1934. Open-fronted ex West Ham Corporation 259 is on route 9 to Stratford; workers are about to board. Note the scissors crossover in the foreground. (G. N. Southerden)

H1 891 leaves for Chingford Mount on route 699. A tram traction standard is retained for street lighting, though it has now gained a trolleybus pole type finial. To those unfamiliar with the surroundings, the area east of the terminus seemed like the back of beyond. (Ken Blacker)

1525 is on its way to Chingford Mount on route 697. The white band on pole number three alerts drivers to the existence of a section insulator at this point – this separates the 'up' and 'down' track. 'Schweppervescence' adverts were seen on London Transport trolleybuses in 1960. (Geoff Bannister)

Even the best laid plans are prone to fail at times and 975 has got it-self out of order on 6th February 1960; another vehicle has over-taken it and 975's poles are being replaced on the overhead prior to its return to Walthamstow depot. To the right 1445 waits out its stand time. (Clarence Carter)

Speeding away from DOCKS and passing the latest arrivals, 1445 is on its way to CROOKED BILLET on route 687 – the rear desti-nation blind has yet to be changed. Having a few minutes layover are Walthamstow's 1107, West Ham's 1666 and an unidentified vehicle. The photographer has captured in one image, the three trolleybus services that terminated here. (Denis Battams)

DOCKS TO PLAISTOW VIA CUSTOM HOUSE

1532 turns from Connaught Road into Prince Regent Lane. Staff pasting 'Buses for Trolleybuses' posters onto traction standards had a long stretch over a steel fence – not that they were read as there is no footpath. An air-raid siren on its own post is operated from within the police call box. Note the sliding ventilators fitted to the nearside upper deck of 1532. (Michael Dryhurst)

On 23rd April 1960 L3 1390 on the 687 is by Winton Road in Victoria Dock Road; the driver is able to 'let her out' on the final approach to DOCKS. It was standard practice for bus stops to be placed opposite each other wherever possible, but the 'stops and signs' department have gone to extreme lengths to do this when preparing for the changeover to motorbuses. The inset reveals that the bus stop post and flag have been placed behind railings and on British Railway's land – how they got an agreement with BR to do this is amazing, but more extraordinary is the fact that staff had to work in close proximity to a working railway line. (Peter Mitchell)

A close-up view of 1518 allows the equipment carried on the roof of a trolleybus to be seen in great detail: trolley gantry, trolley bases, trolley springs, trolley booms, wooden duckboard and retaining hooks. 1518 halts at the compulsory stop outside Custom House station. In the background some prefab houses are in view. (John Wills)

1396 is photographed at Custom House station on its way to DOCKS; the street is devoid of pedestrians and the road absent of other vehicles. It is likely that many of the local gentlemen will visit the barber's and the Custom House hotel in one outing. (Michael Dryhurst)

A fully laden 1432 turns right into Freemasons Road; maybe it is dockers' finishing time as two other trolleybuses follow. 1432 was one of a few vehicles transferred three times during the conversion programme. Stage four: PR/WH. Stage six: WH/HT. Stage ten: HT/FW. Stage fourteen: withdrawn. It was towed away from Fulwell on 21st June 1962 – it had a date with the grim reaper! (Fred Ivey)

At almost the same place as the previous view; 1432's blind is turned for its next trip. Two bikes are propped against the cellar doors of the Railway Tavern; maybe their owners are enjoying a pint of Charrington's Fine Ale. The overhead wires reflect on 1432's offside windscreen on 6th February 1960. (Clarence Carter)

Seen at the junction of Jersey Road with Freemasons Road on 23rd April 1960, L3 1436 is on its way to DOCKS on route 687. This is a barren area as evidenced by the lack of shops and houses; it is quite likely that Freemasons Road suffered heavy bomb damage during the war. (Peter Mitchell)

Seen where New Barn Street meets Beckton Road are two of West Ham's finest -1530 on route 697 heads for Chingford Mount while 1669 on the 687 is not far from DOCKS on 26th March 1960. Both will leave West Ham depot at stage six of the conversion scheme. With fortunes divided, 1530, after a time in store, will go to the scrapman: 1669 will remain in service until 7th November 1961 when it will be at Finchley depot. (Ron Wellings)

E3C class 629C is passing Beeby Road in Beckton Road on 21st April 1956 working on route 697 to Chingford Mount. West Ham depot was not renowned for keeping the paintwork of their vehicles in good external condition, but here 629C looks very smart. (Peter Mitchell)

1395 turns from Beckton Road into New Barn Street while working on the 697; it is 16th April 1960 and trolleybuses will disappear from this point in ten days' time. Note the irregular sett and tarmac road paving arrangement. (Tony Wright)

Turning from New Barn Street into Beckton Road on 23rd April 1960, Walthamstow's 971 nears the end of its journey to DOCKS. Walthamstow changed to Gibson ticket machines on 14th August 1955, far earlier than West Ham who did so on 5th October 1958; there was a time then when passengers were issued with Gibson and Bell punch tickets on the same route on the same day. (Peter Mitchell)

A part of New Barn Street was very narrow, meaning that the gap between the two sets of overhead was minimal by the Army and Navy pub. Heading north on 23rd April 1960, L3 1436 approaches a wider part of the road where the width between the wires gets bigger. Items of note are a missing finial to a traction pole, a barber's dummy and a lady with a wicker shopping basket. (Jack Gready)

'Crooked Billet' was the northern terminus of routes 685/687; they crossed each other here at Abbey Arms. The 685 travelled west/east while the 687 moved south/north; it was quicker and cheaper to travel from 'Abbey Arms' to 'Princess Alice' and beyond by 687. Moving from New Barn Street across Barking Road into Balaam Street 1454 is only going to DOWNSELL ROAD LEYTON. Its last role was to be cannibalised for spare parts. Its final resting place on London Transport property was Colindale depot; a Cohen's wagon would tow it round to the scrapyard behind the depot in October 1961. (Fred Ivey)

M1 1537 passes from Balaam Street into New Barn Street on Good Friday 15th April 1960; it is about to cross Barking Road which is now devoid of trolleybuses. Going the other way, a trolleybus on the 687 heads for the short-working point of Wanstead Flats. (Peter Mitchell)

This view in Balaam Street, on 24th February 1939, is just before its junction with Barking Road; Walthamstow's 339 is on route 697. Trams have now departed from Balaam Street so the Wonderloaf van can be parked on the tram rails without a friendly warning from a tram gong; if a trolleybus going the other way wishes to pass the van it can do so easily. Advertisements appear profusely. Players 'Weights' cigarettes encourage people to purchase their wares, Truman's Ales and Mr Therm are displayed on hoardings and Gent's suede shoes can be bought for under four shillings. Carpets and bedding can be obtained from Staddons while for the canine members of the area, dog cakes and puppy biscuits are on offer. Finally, note the trolleybus bulls-eye next to 339's registration number. (London Transport Museum U29146)

E1 589 has just passed the sewer bank in Balaam Street (by Grange Road) on 6th July 1959. She still uses her original wire grille. VAT 69 whisky is prominently advertised. (Peter Mitchell)

The narrowness of Balaam Street permits the use of a bowstring bracket arm, thus saving the cost of a traction pole; 1548 passes beneath it on 23rd April 1960. The driver is well away from the pavement, giving a wide berth to the elderly gentleman pedalling a three-wheeled invalid carriage. (Jack Gready)

1667 is at the top of Balaam Street, about to turn left into Plaistow High Street; wires to the left allow vehicles to go to and from West Ham depot. 1667 was transferred to Highgate in April 1960; delicensed in March 1961 it was re-activated at Stonebridge in July, remaining in service until 2nd January 1962.

Back at Plaistow Broadway where the 687/697 re-joins the 699; wires to the right lead to West Ham depot. The siting of the frog pull is unusual in being well forward of the turnout; this enables drivers to see their conductors pull the handle down. 1390 heads for DOCKS on the 697. (Fred Ivey)

1442 turns from Plaistow High Street into Balaam Street on 23rd April 1960; the day of reckoning is near as 'Buses for Trolleybuses' posters are pasted onto traction poles. The newsagents shop on the corner of Balaam Street, the 'Coach and Horses' pub and hoarding in the background make people aware of items on sale. Inspectors control trolleybus services and crew changeovers here. (Jack Gready)

Passengers had two options by which to travel between DOCKS and Plaistow Broadway where 1534 on the 699 is seen. It has come via the shorter route than the unidentified 687. (Denis Battams)

A West Ham engineer has brought 624 out as a substitute for 1487 whose rear destination blind has split. A quick change and 624 will be on its way – 1487 will be returned to the depot.

1385 was destroyed in West Ham depot on 30th July 1944; some of its running units were placed on the chassis of 364 whose body had been destroyed at the same time (364 had an ordinary chassis but 1385 was of chassisless construction). With the positioning of the electrical units on the chassis being more in keeping with an N class vehicle it was re-numbered 1385B of class N1B. 1385B passes through the grim Plaistow High Street while working to Chingford Mount on the 699; a non-standard vehicle, it succumbed at stage six of the abandonment programme. It will be parked in Edmonton depot with only a one-way trip to the scrapyard in front of it; although it could have got there under its own power, it suffered the ignominy of being towed by a Cohen's wagon. (Fred Ivey)

TIMES OF FIRST AND LAST TROLLEYBUSES

Route 687   LEYTON DEPOT AND VICTORIA & ALBERT DOCKS, via Wanstead Flats, Balaam Street and New Barn Street

Route 697   CHINGFORD MOUNT AND VICTORIA & ALBERT DOCKS, via Stratford, Balaam Street and New Barn Street

Route 699   CHINGFORD MOUNT AND VICTORIA & ALBERT DOCKS, via Stratford, Greengate Street and Prince Regent Lane

FROM	TO	MONDAY to FRIDAY First (morn.)	MONDAY to FRIDAY Last (night)	SATURDAYS First (morn.)	SATURDAYS Last (night)	SUNDAYS First (morn.)	SUNDAYS Last (night)
Chingford Mount	Leyton (Bakers Arms) ...	5 6	12 21	5 6	12 30	7 36	12 28
	Stratford Broadway ...	5 6	12 21	5 6	12 30	7 36	12 28
	Plaistow Broadway (via Stratford)	5 6	12 21	5 6	12 30	7 36	12 28
	Docks (via Stratford and Balaam Street)	5 6	11 36	5 6	11 31	7 36	11 36
	Docks (via Stratford and Greengate Street)	5 27	11 0	5 27	10 52	9 5	11 13
Leyton (Bakers Arms)	Chingford Mount ...	4 48	12 13	4 48	12 58	7 18	12 22
	Stratford Broadway ...	4 43	12 43	4 43	12 47	7 39*	12 43
	Plaistow Broadway (via Wanstead Flats)	4 56	12 25	4 56	11 31	8 39	11 36
	Plaistow Broadway (via Stratford)	4 43	12 43	4 43	12 47	7 39*	12 43
	Docks (via Wanstead Flats and Balaam Street)	4 56	11 22	4 56	11 31	8 39	11 12
	Docks (via Stratford and Balaam Street)...	4 43	11 51	4 43	11 48	7 39*	11 51
	Docks (via Stratford and Greengate Street)	5 19	11 15	5 19	11 9	8 55	11 28
Leytonstone (Thatched House)	Chingford Mount ...	4 58	12 1	4 58	12 47	8 2	12 11
	Leyton (Bakers Arms) ...	4 58	12 36	4 58	12 47	8 2	12 34
	Stratford Broadway ...	4 53	12 54	4 53	12 58	7 50	12 54
	Plaistow Broadway (via Wanstead Flats)	5 7	12 36	5 7	11 42	8 50	11 47
	Plaistow Broadway (via Stratford)	4 53	12 54	4 53	12 58	7 50	12 54
	Docks (via Wanstead Flats and Balaam Street)	5 7	11 33	5 7	11 42	8 50	11 23
	Docks (via Stratford and Balaam Street)	4 53	12 2	4 53	11 59	7 50	12 2
	Docks (via Stratford and Greengate Street) ...	5 30	11 26	5 30	11 20	9 6	11 39
Plaistow Broadway	Chingford Mount (via Stratford) ...	4 44	11 47	4 44	12 5	7 48	11 57
	Leyton (Bakers Arms) (via Stratford)	4 44	12 22	4 44	12 21	7 48	12 9
	Wanstead Flats ...	5 21	11 49	5 21	11 56	9 32	12 18
	Stratford Broadway ...	4 44	12 22	4 44	12 21	7 48	12 9
	Docks (via Balaam Street)	4 45	12 16	4 45	12 14	7 52	12 16
	Docks (via Greengate Street) ...	5 44	11 40	5 44	11 35	9 20	11 53
Victoria and Albert Docks	Chingford Mount (via New Barn Street and Stratf'd)	4 59	11 26	4 59	11 41	8 6	11 45
	Chingford Mount (via Prince Regent Lane and Stratford) ...	5 23	11 37	5 23	11 55	8 55	11 14
	Leyton (Bakers Arms) (via New Barn St. & Stratf'd)	4 59	12 10	4 59	12 9	8 6	11 57
	Wanstead Flats ...	5 37	11 37	5 46	11 44	9 20	12 6†
	Stratford Broadway (via New Barn Street) ...	4 59	12 10	4 59	12 9	8 6	11 57
	Stratford Broadway (via Greengate Street) ...	5 23	11 52	5 23	11 55	8 55	11 50
	Plaistow Broadway (via New Barn Street) ...	4 59	12 10	4 59	12 9	8 6	12 6
	Greengate Street Depot (via Prince Regent Lane)	5 23	11 52	5 23	11 55	6 54	12 29
	Plaistow (Abbey Arms)...	4 59	12 30	4 59	12 30	8 6	12 6

* From Walthamstow (Crooked Billet) 7.27 a.m.   † To Bakers Arms.

SERVICE INTERVALS

BETWEEN	MON.-FRI. Peak (mins.)	MON.-FRI. Normal (mins.)	SATURDAYS Peak (mins.)	SATURDAYS Normal (mins.)	SUNDAYS Morn. (mins.)	SUNDAYS Aftn. (mins.)
Leyton (Bakers Arms) and Docks (via Wanstead Flats)	6	6	6	6	8	6
Chingford Mount and Docks (via Stratford and Balaam Street) ...	6	6	6	6	8	6
Chingford Mount and Docks (via Stratford and Greengate Street) ...	6	6	6	6	8	6
" Greengate " and Docks...	2	6	2	4	8	
Plaistow Broadway and Docks ...	2	3	1½	3	6	3

ON PUBLIC HOLIDAYS trolleybuses run at special times which are advertised in the vehicles

★ GREEN LINE COACH GUIDE

TWOPENCE

From coach conductors or newsagents

ABBey 1234   61   11th June, 1939

Waterlow & Sons Limited, London & Dunstable

Working on route 687, E2 628 and L3 1401 are outside the 'Black Lion' in Plaistow High Street on Saturday 21st February 1959; the older of the two vehicles has all its lights on. With no scheduled workings to Wanstead Flats on the 687 in daytime, 628 is running late and has been curtailed well short of its Crooked Billet destination. Plenty of 'waiting time' for the crew! 1401 is working the full length of the route. There was no 'class distinction' on the 687. (Allen Smith, courtesy Alan Cross)

Heading north in Plaistow High Street, a well-laden 887 bumps over the setts on its way to Chingford Mount on route 699. Red and White Cigarettes and Vernons Pools are advertised, encouraging people to fritter their money away. Feeder cables are set well back from the roadway. (Ron Wellings)

Plaistow suffered from heavy bombing – the building on the right and seen on page 24 may have been a victim of the conflict. 1536 pauses at Clegg Street junction; although a bus stop is not positioned here, passengers alight while the conductor goes for the frog pull. The second traction standard on the left had been erected in preparation for an abortive attempt to widen Plaistow High Street. As can be seen, the narrow section of the High Street, which raised concerns with the Ministry of Transport inspector and which required a system of trolleybus lights, was very short. (Robert Jowitt)

Wednesday 7th December, 1949

        10.17 a.m. Clegg St., junction with High St., Plaistow.
Adjusting bar of pull frog damaged by dewirement.
                                    12 mins. Passenger delay.
                                18 "   Electrical delay.

PLAISTOW TO CANNING TOWN

596 turns into Upper Road on 9th July 1959 while working on the 669. Behind, and on the inside track, H1 800 heads south on the 697. E1 596 spent its life working at West Ham depot; H1 800 is a newcomer to the area having worked at Bexleyheath depot for most of its life. (John Clarke)

A sound looking 575C is at the top end of Upper Road on its way to North Woolwich on route 669. The driver has not positioned the destination blind very well, for although North Woolwich is indicated, it is not showing the rest of the display which was 'VIA CANNING TOWN'. (Ron Wellings)

Seen by Grange Road in Upper Road on 21st April 1956, E2 615 heads for North Woolwich. There is no other vehicle in sight; at the time, many people depended on public transport. (Peter Mitchell)

E2 620 is seen by Hermit Road recreation ground on 21st April 1956. Much of this part of East London at this time was on cobbled roads; however slowly a driver passed over them, there would have been a little bit of discomfort to passengers. (Peter Mitchell)

M1 1544 is by Bethell Avenue on Hermit Road on the last Saturday of operation of the 669 – 30th January 1960. The grimness of the day is exacerbated by the heavy duty feeders and the dingy-looking houses. (Peter Mitchell)

Traction standards with bowstring arms were used extensively in the East End; presumably it was a cost saving exercise as Upper Road was wide enough to support overhead by conventional means. 1456 is on its way to North Woolwich and passes the Marquis of Salisbury public house by Blake Road in Hermit Road. Prominent, are telegraph wires fitted to traction poles.

71

1401 is on a '685 short' that starts at Canning Town; it is 4.46pm on 9th July 1959 and 1401 waits in Cliff Street. The photographer describes the two turning circles here as North loop and South loop (he was cognizant of this terminology at the Pier Head terminus of Liverpool trams); this is north loop. In the background, houses will soon be demolished. (John Clarke)

At the bottom of Hermit Road, two 669s pass each other; 606 heads south to North Woolwich while 1405 makes its way to Stratford Broadway on 29th September 1959. Redevelopment is taking place at Canning Town, replacing slum areas in the vicinity. The policeman on point duty has a white gaiter over each of his arms. (John Clarke)

Moving from Hermit Road into Barking Road at Canning Town is E1 580. Traffic lights have not been installed here and the policeman on duty gives 580 priority over vehicles moving west along Barking Road; one that is held is a 665 on its way to Clerkenwell Green. Additional illumination (supplied by the local council for safety reasons) is given by means of a lamp mounted to pole 205 (just below the frog pull wire) and another on the other side of the road. The view shows all three items of special work here. (Fred Ivey)

L3 1382 on the 690 waits on Stratford Broadway stand which was predominantly used by vehicles on routes 669, 689 and 690; it was principally used by vehicles operating out of West Ham depot. The only time that other routes and another depot might use it were late running 697s and 699s from Walthamstow and West Ham depots. Passing by on route 661 to Aldgate is N1 1637. (Marcus Eavis, courtesy Online Transport Archive)

Walthamstow depot operated a number of H1s – one was 887 which is in Tramway Avenue Stratford, on its way to Victoria and Albert Docks on route 699. This was the main loading point for southbound trolleybuses at this location. (London Transport Museum)

ON & AFTER JUNE 6

TROLLEYBUS ROUTE 687

will operate between

Chingford Mount & Victoria & Albert Docks

(via Wanstead Flats, Abbey Arms & New Barn St.)

Tram Route 87

will be withdrawn

Times of First and Last Trolleybuses		MONDAY TO FRIDAY		SATURDAY		SUNDAY	
		FIRST	LAST	FIRST	LAST	FIRST	LAST
		Morning	Night	Morning	Night	Morning	Night
Chingford Mount to							
Leyton (Baker's Arms)... ...		6 35	11 39	6 35	11 5	9 0	11 20
Plaistow Broadway		6 35	11 39	6 35	11 5	9 0	11 20
Victoria & Albert Docks ...		6 35	11 39	6 35	11 1	9 0	11 8
Leyton (Baker's Arms) to							
Chingford Mount		5 50	12 13	5 48	11 49	8 43	11 43
Plaistow Broadway		4 56	11 54	4 56	11 20	8 39	11 35
Victoria & Albert Docks ...		4 56	10 59	4 56	11 16	8 39	11 23
Wanstead Flats to							
Chingford Mount		5 33	11 56	5 31	11 32	9 42	11 26
Leyton (Baker's Arms)... ...		5 33	12 5	5 31	11 50	9 42	12 26
Plaistow Broadway		5 13	12 11	5 13	11 37	8 56	11 52
Victoria & Albert Docks ...		5 13	11 31	5 13	11 33	8 56	11 40
Plaistow Broadway to							
Chingford Mount		5 23	11 46	5 21	11 22	9 32	11 16
Leyton (Baker's Arms)... ...		5 23	11 55	5 21	11 40	9 32	12 16
Victoria & Albert Docks ...		5 23	11 41	5 23	11 43	9 6	11 50
Victoria & Albert Docks to							
Chingford Mount		5 34	11 34	5 40	11 10	9 20	11 4
Leyton (Baker's Arms)... ...		5 34	11 43	5 40	11 28	9 20	12 4
Plaistow Broadway		5 34	11 43	5 40	11 28	9 20	12 4

Service Interval : 5—6 minutes

ON & AFTER JUNE 6
TROLLEYBUS ROUTE 697
will operate between
Chingford Mount and
Victoria & Albert Docks
(via Stratford, Abbey Arms & New Barn Street)
Tram Route 97
will be withdrawn

Times of First and Last Trolleybuses

	MONDAY TO FRIDAY		SATURDAY		SUNDAY	
	FIRST	LAST	FIRST	LAST	FIRST	LAST
	Morning	Night	Morning	Night	Morning	Night
Chingford Mount to						
Leyton (Baker's Arms)	5 9	12 19	5 9	12 40	7 36	12 20
Plaistow Broadway	5 9	12 19	5 9	11 38	7 36	12 20
Victoria & Albert Docks ...	5 9	11 33	5 9	11 33	7 36	11 36
Leyton (Baker's Arms) to						
Chingford Mount	4 51	11 26	4 52	12 12	7 18	12 19
Plaistow Broadway	5 24	12 43	5 24	12 43	7 51	12 35
Victoria & Albert Docks ...	5 24	11 48	5 24	11 48	7 51	11 51
Stratford Broadway to						
Chingford Mount	5 18	11 9	5 20	11 55	8 21	12 2
Plaistow Broadway	5 3	1 0	5 3	1 0	8 8	12 52
Victoria & Albert Docks ...	5 3	12 5	5 3	12 5	8 8	12 8
Plaistow Broadway to						
Chingford Mount	5 10	11 1	5 12	11 47	8 13	11 54
Leyton (Baker's Arms) ...	5 5	12 16	5 5	12 15	8 13	11 54
Victoria & Albert Docks ...	4 48	12 13	4 46	12 13	7 52	12 16
Victoria & Albert Docks to						
Chingford Mount	5 2	10 49	5 0	11 35	8 6	11 42
Plaistow Broadway	5 2	12 4	5 0	12 9	8 6	11 55

Service Interval 5–6 minutes.

37—2515—275/2 chgs.

STAFF PROBLEMS AT PLAISTOW BROADWAY

Plaistow Broadway was the crew relief point for West Ham staff working on routes 687 and 697 (crews on the 699 changed over outside the depot). (Top) 1668 on the 697 is the victim of a 'staff cut' and is being run into the depot; the conductor has failed to change the rear blind from DOCKS to WEST HAM DEPOT – not very professional! (Lower) Two trolleybuses have arrived from Prince Regent Lane, but why the leading vehicle, 1455, shows 697 is mysterious as it should have travelled via Custom House. The driver walks away and follows an inspector who maybe is in despair that it has travelled from Docks via the 699. The following vehicle is a 'true' 699. (London Transport Museum)

Seen in Balaam Street, E1 599 is working on route 697 to DOCKS on Tuesday 29th September 1959. At 1.31pm, the scene is devoid of pedestrians and vehicles. (John Clarke)

The L3s allocated to West Ham depot saw a lot of service on 'Docks' routes. Having just left the Connaught Road terminus of Victoria and Albert Docks, 1437 performs another journey on the 699 to Chingford Mount. 9th January 1960 was a dull day. (John Clarke)

On Silverton Way three trolleybuses are seen in the winter sunshine of 5th December 1959. On the right is 1432 working south to Silvertown on route 685. On the left 1398 on the 669 follows 627 which is a 685 heading for WALTHAMSTOW SINNOTT ROAD. 627 is only a short way into its northbound trip but an inspector has noticed it is already running late and has consequently taken remedial action to turn it short of Crooked Billet. (John Clarke)

The concrete arches of Silvertown flyover were a significant landmark in East London. Leaving the edifice, on 9th January 1960, M1 1538 heads for North Woolwich on route 669. (John Clarke)

The E class vehicles that were allocated to West Ham depot were predominantly seen on 'Docks services'. This also applied to the rebodied E classes allocated there; 639C is photographed in very grim surroundings just east of Silvertown, while working on route 669. (Phil Tatt, courtesy Online Transport Archive)

L3 1437 has just left the North Woolwich terminus and is turning into Pier Road, working to Stratford Broadway. This vehicle had been resident at Poplar depot from new so would have seen North Woolwich many times while operating on route 569. On 1st June 1959 it was transferred to West Ham so would have spent many a day working on the 669 – it is very likely that it would have also been seen here on the 685.

The main trolleybus route to serve West India Docks was the 677. Seen at Ming Street terminus is K1 1299 which will soon be off on a trip to Smithfield. (Marcus Eavis, courtesy Online Transport Archive)

L3 1442 passes through Gardiners Corner on 31st October 1959 working on route 665 to Barking. At the moment the complex overhead layout is complete, but once the 567/569/665 services run for the last time on 10th November 1959, much of the wiring will be removed. (John Clarke)

Both of 1523's poles have left the overhead on the trailing frog at Hermit Road; it has come to a standstill a few yards further on. It would be understandable if a 669 had come to grief coming round the corner, so 1523 has been driven through the junction a bit too quickly. Note how far back traction standard five is from the main road. Those sticking 'Buses for Trolleybuses' posters on traction standards have not even failed to miss this one – obviously dedicated employees! (Tony Belton)

For much of the trolleybus era, older classes of trolleybuses were allocated to route 669 – with the reduction of services and the withdrawal of vehicles at West Ham depot, some newer vehicles made an appearance on this route. N2 1659 is in Canning Town. (Fred Ivey)

Passing Canning Town synagogue, 1500 is not far from TRINITY CHURCH CANNING TOWN. The hoardings on the right are typical of the late 1950s; adverts for 'The Used Car Show' date this view as October 1959. London Transport liked rainy days as it put bums on seats. (Michael Dryhurst)

COMMENDATIONS

Mr. J. W. LOCK
Conductor No. T.9318
Poplar Depot

19, Girdwood Road,
London, S.W.18.

Dear Sir,

I had occasion to make a journey on business from here to Beckton Road and was advised to go to Aldgate East and then take a bus at Gardiners Corner.

A No. 567 came along, No. FXH 503, and I asked the Conductor T.9318 as to direction and was told to get aboard and he would tell me when he came up for fares. This he did, telling me to get off at Canning Town Station and wait at the stop for a 175 or 160 (Becontree) which would take me right along Beckton Road and mentioned the stop by the Park which I should get off for Freemasons Road.

Not only to myself was he most helpful, but also to other passengers in the bus and it is a pleasure to record this. I don't know the man from Adam, but such servants are a credit to the travelling public. I have had the other sort of treatment and appreciate the difference. I took the numbers on my own so that the employee may be checked upon, and he did not know I had done this.

Yours faithfully,
(Signed) N. C. HEADLAND.

LETTERS OF COMMENDATION HAVE ALSO BEEN RECEIVED REGARDING:

Mr. H. J. AYTON	...	Driver	... No. T.7952	...	Walthamstow Depot.
Mr. W. B. BARRATT	...	Conductor	... No. 11971	...	Stonebridge Depot.
Mr. A. E. BUNCE	...	Conductor	... No. T.12931	...	Walthamstow Depot.
Miss H. R. HINDS	...	W/Conductor	... No. 12559	...	New Cross Depot.
MR. G. H. ROBINSON		Driver	... No. 8697	...	Stonebridge Depot.
Mr. L. R. SIMMONS	...	Inspector	... —	...	Bexleyheath Depot.

COMPLAINT

I desire to call to your attention the conduct of one of your Trolleybus Conductors on the —— to —— service.

I was about to board the bus this morning at the —— Stopping Point when the conductor gave the signal to proceed while I had my hand on the rail, the time would be about 7.25. On my drawing the attention of the conductor that his bus was not stationary he began to abuse me by telling me that I should be at the stop in time, drawing attention to the regulation as laid down. He did not want to be told what he was to do. On the conductor coming up for the fares he again used words of abuse, finishing with the words that I could go and —— myself, with that I said I would have his Badge No. He said that I could have it there and then, anyway on leaving the bus I took the number which is No. —— also the number of ticket issued to me is ——.

It is not the first time this has happened, but I have refrained from making a complaint owing to circumstances which we have gone through, but it is time that attention was drawn to the conductors, and drivers as well, on this route, that time is allowed for passengers to board the bus at the stopping places.

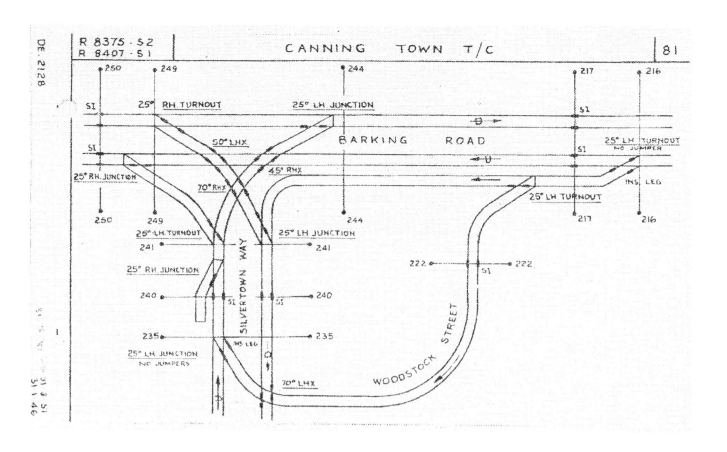

1710.—EXTENSION OF ROUTE 669 TO NORTH WOOLWICH (FREE FERRY).

Notice to Inspectors and Conductors—West Ham Depot.

On Sunday, 6th February, 1938, Route 669 was extended to operate between Stratford Broadway and North Woolwich (Free Ferry).

TICKETS.

Tickets containing the necessary sections for use on the new extension have been in use since September, 1937, so that conductors should now be familiar with them.

WORKMAN TICKETS

Workman tickets will be issued on the new extension on all trolleybuses up to 8.0 a.m. and after this time until arrival at the next farestage point.

GENERAL.

1/- All-day, 6d. All-day Child's and 6d. Tourist (Northern area) tickets will be available over the new extension.

1691.—ROUTE 669—OVERHEAD FROG—BARKING ROAD AT WOODSTOCK STREET.

On and after Sunday, 6th February, this frog will be set for the straight run into Silvertown Way—pull for buses to enter Woodstock Street.

Apart from depots, there were few places on the system where two frog pulls were almost together for any manoeuvre. One was at Canning Town where the turn from Woodstock Street was followed by one into Silvertown Way (see map). The frog into Woodstock Street is in the foreground. This photograph was taken on 17th October 1959. (John Gillham)

606 is in Woodstock Street in the early 1950s; all its blinds were made at Charlton. To efficiently run a service, running numbers denoted the order of each vehicle in the schedule; 606 is WH3/685. However, there were a number of WH3s on the road at any one time; this confusing arrangement which occurred at most depots was later rationalised to avoid duplication. (London County Council Tramways Trust)

Three 685s are in Woodstock Street; identifiable are M1 1536 and E3 636. OMO washing powder outnumbers Ben Truman's adverts by two to one; 1536's front offside advert has been torn away and a disgrace to the high standards usually set. 1536 works short to Wanstead Flats. (Alan Cross)

There is a problem on the Barking Road routes as 665s are turning in Woodstock Street. In the top view, Poplar's 1518 cannot show a plain 'CANNING TOWN' display without any amplification so TRINITY CHURCH CANNING TOWN suffices. Assuming that there will be some time to wait, the crew of 1518 have dropped their poles, which courteously allows 685s to pass freely. In the lower picture West Ham's 1596 shows a plain CANNING TOWN. (Tony Belton)

The grimness of an East London trolleybus turning loop is illustrated by this view of Woodstock Street in Canning Town on 16th February 1960. This was exactly two weeks after the last 685 had used these wires. The last trolley – 969 on WH 35 – had gone. (Hugh Taylor)

1099 is off to WALTHAMSTOW CROOKED BILLET; the driver shows this display rather than the correct one which incorporated via points. Maybe 1099 is running into Walthamstow depot and means that when he reaches Crooked Billet the driver will only have a short wind of the blind handle to show DEPOT WALTHAMSTOW. Houses in Woodstock Street were demolished as part of the East End slum clearances. The 'Woodstock Arms' and J. Thrake at number 26 survived the war. (Fred Ivey)

1546 is outside the 'Woodstock Arms'; most 685 trips to Wanstead Flats occurred on Saturdays. RM41 on the 238 is working to BECONTREE CHITTYS LANE; the route was introduced at stage four of the conversion scheme – it did not replace a trolleybus service but was a new initiative. (Fred Ivey)

Re-bodied 578C is by Fox Street in Woodstock Street on 21st April 1956. It shows Canning Town, implying that there has not been a crew to take it over at the relief point here. To the right, slum clearance has taken place and the area is now wasteland. (Peter Mitchell)

CANNING TOWN TO NORTH WOOLWICH

A few trips on the 685 only went as far as to the little-used loop at FINDEN ROAD GREEN STREET; 1663 turns from Silvertown Way into Barking Road on one such journey The number blind has slipped – either the blind mechanism is worn or the conductor has failed to set it properly. (Fred Ivey)

On 10th November 1959, West Ham's 1539 is on tuition duties. It is the last day of routes 567/569/665 so it will be pointless for trainees to turn left here. (Brian Speller)

New Route 569—Aldgate and Silvertown Station

Notice to Inspectors and Conductors—Poplar Depot

Commencing on Wednesday, 23rd July, a new route numbered 569 will operate during peak hours only between Aldgate and Silvertown Station, via Silvertown Way.

Fares

Fares for journeys to and from points east of Canning Town Station are :—

Journey.	Ordinary Single	Work-man Return	Journey	Ordinary Single	Work-man Return
	d.	*d.*	8 Burdett Road and 12 Royal Victoria Dock Entrance	2	2½
5 Aldgate and 11 Tidal Basin Road	3	—	8 Burdett Road and 14 Silvertown Station	3	4
5 Aldgate and 13 Graving Dock Tavern	4	4	9 Blackwall Tunnel and 11 Tidal Basin Road	1½	—
5 Aldgate and 14 Silvertown Station	5	6	9 Blackwall Tunnel and 13 Graving Dock Tavern	2	2½
6 New Road and 12 Royal Victoria Dock Entrance	3	—	10 Canning Town and 12 Royal Victoria Dock Entrance	1½	—
6 New Road and 14 Silvertown Station	4	4	10 Canning Town and 14 Silvertown Station	2	2½
7 Stepney Station and 11 Tidal Basin Road	2	2½	11 Tidal Basin Road and 15 Graving Dock Tavern	1½	—
7 Stepney Station and 13 Graving Dock Tavern	3	—	12 Royal Victoria Dock Entrance and 14 Silvertown Station	1½	—

Cheap Midday Fares

5 Aldgate and 10 Canning Town Station ..   2*d.*

5   „   and 12 Royal Victoria Dock Entrance   ..   ..   ..   3½*d.*

5   „   and 14 Silvertown Station   ..   4*d.*

1/- Day Ticket

The 1*s.* day ticket is available throughout the new route.

Transfers

A transfer on the return journey at Canning Town Station is provided for passengers making return workman journeys through that point when Route 669 is not operating. A special section is provided on workman tickets, and tickets presented for transfer must be cancelled in this section on the edge opposite to the punch hole.

Copies of the revised farebill and specimens of altered tickets will be exhibited in the depot.

Blinds

The following wordings have been added to the blinds and must be shown :—

When running to	Front and Rear		Side		Number
	No.		No.		
Silvertown Station ..	11A	SILVERTOWN STATION Via Canning Town and Commercial Road, ALDGATE	7	Commercial Road .. .. East India Dock Road .. Canning Town .. .. Silvertown Way	569
Aldgate	10				

Approved—

T. E. THOMAS,
    General Manager (Operation),
      London Passenger Transport Board,
        55, Broadway, S.W.1.

7th July, 1941.

S. R. GEARY,
    Operating Manager
      (Trams and Trolleybuses).

195

LONDON TRANSPORT
TRAFFIC CIRCULAR
TRAMS & TROLLEYBUSES
No. 169

In operation on and from 17th October, 1941, unless otherwise stated.

Extension of Route 569 — 2814

Notice to Inspectors and Conductors—
Poplar Depot

Commencing on Wednesday, 29th October, Route No. 569 now operating between Aldgate and Silvertown Station during peak hours will be extended to operate between Aldgate and North Woolwich Free Ferry. Fares for journeys to points east of Silvertown Station are:—

Journey.	Ordinary Single	Workman Return
	d.	d.
5 Aldgate and 15 Albert Road, Henley Arms	5	—
5 Aldgate and 16 North Woolwich Free Ferry	6	6
6 New Road and 16 North Woolwich Free Ferry	5	5
7 Stepney Station and 15 Albert Road, Henley Arms	4	4
8 Burdett Road and 16 North Woolwich Free Ferry	4	4
9 Blackwall Tunnel and 15 Albert Road, Henley Arms	3	—
10 Canning Town Station and 16 North Woolwich Free Ferry	3	3
11 Tidal Basin Road and 15 Albert Road, Henley Arms	2	$2\frac{1}{2}$
12 Royal Victoria Dock and 16 North Woolwich Free Ferry	2	$2\frac{1}{2}$
13 Graving Dock Tavern and 15 Albert Road, Henley Arms	$1\frac{1}{2}$	—
14 Silvertown Station and 16 North Woolwich Free Ferry	$1\frac{1}{2}$	—

Midday Fare

Aldgate and North Woolwich Free Ferry .. 5d.

1/- Day Ticket

The 1s. day ticket is available to North Woolwich.

Copies of the revised farebill and specimens of altered tickets will be exhibited in the depot. Attention is drawn to the new style numbered $2\frac{1}{2}d.$ workman return ticket.

Destination Blind

An addition to the front and rear blinds has been made, and when running to Woolwich Free Ferry the following wording must be shown:—

> 11B NORTH WOOLWICH
> via Commercial Road
> and Silvertown Way

Transfers

A transfer on the return journey at Canning Town Station is provided for passengers making return workman journeys through that point when Route 569 is not operating. A special section is provided on workman tickets, and tickets presented for transfer must be cancelled in this section on the edge opposite to the punch hole.

Women Conductors — 2815

Lavatory and Washing Facilities

Additions—

The Bee Café, Bournes Corner, Plaistow.
Public Convenience, Islington Green.

214

1495 has suffered a dewirement at Canning Town and has the services of a breakdown gang who are straightening the bent booms – one man is on the roof while another stands in the emergency exit. Traditionally in London, a way of indicating that a vehicle is disabled was to prop a seat against the back; in this case, a crew member uses a newsvendor's 'Evening Star' placard. 1392's next driver will have to put the steering wheel on full lock to get by. Note the close proximity of the parking wires' trailing frog and the facing frog at the top of Silvertown Way. (Michael Dryhurst)

Time has moved on and stage four of the conversion scheme has taken place; this is indicated by the removal of the facing frog at the top of Silvertown Way. 979's blind is halfway between two displays (CANNING TOWN and VICTORIA DOCKS), this was common practice when working 669 'shorts' between Trinity Church and Victoria Docks – it saved blind winding. (Michael Dryhurst)

The wide Silvertown Way is shown to good effect in this view taken on 30th January 1960. 1666 is only going to Wanstead Flats on route 685; on the shunt wire behind, a 669 is out of service. It looks as if 627 on the 669 on the opposite side of the road is also devoid of a crew as it is showing CANNING TOWN; if that is so it will soon have its poles dropped. (Ron Wellings)

West Ham depot operated a number of J2s from 1954; a later arrival was 963 which came in January 1959 – it is seen at the top of Silvertown Way. 963 is stopping here at Canning Town. Adjacent to it is a trolleybus rescue tender which has been assisting in the locality. (Ron Lunn)

The Park Royal bodied E3s were a constant cause for concern – despite refurbishment in the early post-war period, they continued to deteriorate with the result that all were withdrawn by October 1956. E3 648 is on the parking wire at the top end of Silvertown Way. Crewless, it shows 669 STRATFORD BROADWAY, indicating that it has been taken out of service at the last moment. (Alan Cross)

The lack of traffic at Canning Town indicates a Sunday view; turning from Barking Road into Silvertown Way is 1460. In the background, two cooling towers can be seen. (Don Thompson)

In November 1959, London Transport staff dismantled redundant wires at Canning Town junction; all that is left are wires from Barking Road into Silvertown Way. It is now an easy path for drivers heading down Silvertown Way as exemplified by 1433 on route 669 on 30th January 1960. (Ron Wellings)

J1 973 is at the top of Silvertown Way. When destination blinds were made at Charlton Works there was a VICTORIA DOCKS VIA SILVERTOWN WAY & CANNING TOWN display. When production moved to Aldenham the via and ampersand were not incorporated. (Fred Ivey)

It would appear that E1 577 has broken down at the top of Silvertown Way as a service vehicle is parked behind. Of note is the destination blind which incorporates a panel made at Chiswick Works and therefore of motorbus style. The date is 21st April 1956. (Peter Mitchell)

1400 turns out of Woodstock Street while working on route 685. Much of the service only went as far as Wanstead Flats on Saturdays so as to accommodate heavy passenger use on this section. (L. Nicholson, courtesy Transport Treasury)

Comparing this view to the previous one, it will be observed that demolition has recently taken place at the bottom end of Woodstock Street; against a now desolate background, 1448 passes the crossover here. Moving from Poplar to West Ham depot in November 1959, it is in familiar territory. Between 1943 and 1949, Woodstock Street was part of a turning facility for trolleybuses working short from the Silvertown direction; these manoeuvres required a left hand turn from Woodstock Street into Silvertown Way. It was one of a few instances of passengers being carried in battery mode. (Fred Ivey)

Wednesday, 24th January, 1951

      11.20 p.m. Green Lanes Palmers Green.   Damage to overhead equipment caused by lorry with high load.   Further damage caused by same lorry at 5.15 a.m. the following morning in Silvertown Way, North Woolwich, causing dislocation of Trolleybus Services.

                              20 mins. Passenger delay.

- 2 -

ROAD POWER SERVICES - TROLLEYBUSES (CONTD.)

Easter Monday 10th April, 1950

      1.15 p.m. West Ham Area.   Failure of H.T. supply from L.E.B., shut down Canning Town, Prince Regent Lane, Greengate Street, Church Street, Forest Gate Substations for 40 minutes, and Silvertown Substation for 95 minutes.
                        Passenger delays 40 and
                              95 minutes.

N2 1667 is working on route 669 to North Woolwich; span wire configuration is about to change to tubular pole construction. It was a relatively easy task for Cohens (the scrap merchants) to remove ordinary standards; to dismantle those with bracket arms was more difficult. Today, second-hand cars are usually sold from large sites: in the late 'fifties this type of business was run from small car lots – one is adjacent to 1667. (Norman Rayfield)

Silvertown Way was opened by Minister of Transport, Leslie Hore Belisha (well known for his work on pedestrian crossings) on 13th September 1934. Some conductors were rather tardy in their workmanship, for 622 having previously operated on route 699, has yet to have its blinds changed to show 669 and whatever destination it is going to. It left West Ham depot some time ago so the blinds should have been changed by now. (Norman Rayfield)

FARES
SILVERTOWN & WALTHAMSTOW

ROUTE 685

The fare chart below is a triangular table. For each station row the fares are listed from left to right, beginning with the fare from Stage Point 3 (Silvertown Station) and continuing up to the adjacent stage. The three left-hand columns give fares from West Ham L.T. Depot (32), North Woolwich Free Ferry (1) and Albert Road, Henley Arms (2).

West Ham L.T. Depot 32	N. Woolwich Free Ferry 1	Albert Road, Henley Arms 2	Stage Point No.	Station	Fares (from Stage 3 → adjacent stage)
	3		3	SILVERTOWN STATION 3	—
	3	3	4	GRAVING DOCK TAVERN 4	3
	4	3	5	ROYAL VICTORIA DOCK ENTRANCE 5	3 3
	5	4	6	TIDAL BASIN ROAD 6	4 3 3
	7	5	7	CANNING TOWN STATION 7	5 4 3 3
	7	7	8	BARKING ROAD, Beckton Road 8	7 5 4 3 3
	9	7	9	BALAAM STREET 9	7 7 5 4 3 3
3	9	9	10	GREENGATE STREET 10	7 7 5 4 3 3 3
3	11	11	11	GREEN STREET, Barking Road 11	9 8 7 6 4 4 3 3
4	11	11	12	UPTON PARK STATION 12	9 9 7 7 5 4 4 3 3
4	11	11	13	PLASHET ROAD 13	9 9 7 7 5 5 4 3 3 3
5	1/1	1/1	14	STUDLEY ROAD 14	11 11 9 8 7 7 5 4 3 3 3
5	1/1	1/1	15	ROMFORD ROAD, Woodgrange Road 15	11 11 9 9 7 7 7 5 4 3 3 3
7	1/3	1/3	16	WANSTEAD FLATS, Forest Road 16	1/1 1/1 11 11 9 8 7 7 5 4 4 3 3
7	1/3	1/3	17	WOODHOUSE ROAD 17	1/1 1/1 11 11 9 9 7 7 7 5 5 4 3 3
9	1/5	1/5	18	LEYTONSTONE, Thatched House 18	1/3 1/3 1/1 1/1 11 11 9 9 7 7 7 5 4 3 3
9	1/5	1/5	19	TEMPLE MILLS LANE 19	1/3 1/3 1/1 1/1 11 11 9 9 9 7 7 7 5 4 3 3
9	1/5	1/5	20	LEYTON L.T. STATION 20	1/3 1/3 1/1 1/1 11 11 9 9 9 7 7 7 5 4 3 3 3
11	1/7	1/7	21	HIGH ROAD, Grange Park Road 21	1/5 1/5 1/3 1/3 1/1 1/1 11 11 9 9 9 7 7 5 4 3 3 3
11	1/7	1/7	22	CRESCENT ROAD, Osborn Arms 22	1/5 1/5 1/3 1/3 1/1 1/1 11 11 11 9 9 9 7 7 5 4 4 3 3
1/1	1/9	1/9	23	LEA BRIDGE ROAD, Markhouse Road 23	1/7 1/7 1/5 1/5 1/3 1/3 1/1 1/1 11 11 11 9 9 7 7 5 5 4 3 3
1/1	1/9	1/9	24	QUEENS ROAD 24	1/7 1/7 1/5 1/5 1/3 1/3 1/1 1/1 1/1 11 11 11 9 9 7 7 7 5 4 3 3
1/3	1/11	1/11	25	ST. JAMES STREET STATION 25	1/9 1/9 1/7 1/7 1/5 1/5 1/3 1/3 1/3 1/1 1/1 1/1 11 11 9 9 7 7 7 5 4 3
1/3	1/11	1/11	26	STANDARD JUNCTION 26	1/9 1/9 1/7 1/7 1/5 1/5 1/3 1/3 1/3 1/1 1/1 1/1 11 11 9 9 9 7 7 5 4 3 3
1/5	2/–	2/–	27	GLOUCESTER ROAD 27	1/11 1/11 1/9 1/9 1/7 1/7 1/5 1/5 1/5 1/3 1/3 1/3 1/1 1/1 11 11 9 9 9 7 7 5 4 3 3
1/5	2/–	2/–	28	HIGHAM HILL ROAD 28	1/11 1/11 1/9 1/9 1/7 1/7 1/5 1/5 1/5 1/3 1/3 1/3 1/1 1/1 11 11 11 9 9 7 7 5 4 3 3
1/7	2/2	2/2	29	NORTH COUNTESS ROAD 29	2/– 2/– 1/11 1/11 1/9 1/9 1/7 1/7 1/5 1/5 1/5 1/3 1/3 1/1 1/1 11 11 11 9 9 7 7 5 4 3 3
1/7	2/2	2/2	30	WALTHAMSTOW, Crooked Billet 30	2/– 2/– 1/11 1/11 1/9 1/9 1/7 1/7 1/7 1/5 1/5 1/5 1/3 1/3 1/1 1/1 1/1 11 11 9 9 7 7 5 4 3 3
			31	WALTHAMSTOW L.T. DEPOT 31	2/2 2/2 2/– 2/– 1/11 1/11 1/9 1/9 1/7 1/7 1/7 1/5 1/5 1/3 1/3 1/1 1/1 1/1 11 11 9 9 7 7 5 4 3 3
			32	WEST HAM L.T. DEPOT 32	9 7 7 5 4 3 3 3

434 (1959)

FARES FOR CHILDREN
under 14 years of age

One child under 3 years of age accompanied by a fare paying passenger and not occupying a seat, is carried free. Additional children under 3 years and all children of 3 years and under 14 years of age are carried at half the adult single fare, fractions of 1d. charged as 1d.

EARLY MORNING SINGLE FARES

Available daily for journeys started at or after 3 a.m. and finishing at or before 8 a.m. In the case of journeys started before and finishing after 8 a.m., early morning fares will be available only to the stage point at which this vehicle is scheduled to be at 8 a.m. Tickets issued to children at the adult fare only.

Where the Ordinary Single Fare is	Early Morning Single fare will be
1/1d.—1/9d.	1/–d.
1/11d.	1/2d.
2/–d.—2/2d.	1/3d.

Early Morning Single tickets issued from some ticket issuing machines will show "A" for the 1/–d. fare in the "Fare Paid" space.

TIMES OF FIRST AND LAST TROLLEYBUSES
Route 685

WALTHAMSTOW (CROOKED BILLET) AND CANNING TOWN

Extended during weekday peak hours to Silvertown Station via Silvertown Way

FROM	TO	MONDAYS to FRIDAYS First (morn.)	MONDAYS to FRIDAYS Last (night)	SATURDAYS First (morn.)	SATURDAYS Last (night)	SUNDAYS First (morn.)	SUNDAYS Last (night)
Walthamstow (Crooked Billet)	Leyton (Markhouse Road) ...	5 8	12 11	5 8	12 22	8 45	12 11
	Upton Park (Boleyn) ...	5 29	12 11	5 29	12 22	8 45	12 11
	Canning Town ...	5 29	11 7	5 29	11 3	8 45	10 59
	Royal Victoria Docks (Clyde Road) Morn.	5 29	8 6a.m.	5 29	8 2a.m.	—	—
	Even.	3 21p.m.	6 1p.m.	10 42	1 3Aft.	—	—
	Silvertown Station Morn.	6 1	8 0a.m.	6 1	8 2a.m.	—	—
	Even.	3 21	5 54	10 50	1257Aft.	—	—
Walthamstow (Royal Standard)	Walthamstow (Crooked Billet) ...	5 16	12 15	5 16	12 13	8 33	11 56
	Leyton (Markhouse Road)	5 18	12 19	5 18	12 31	8 53	12 20
	Upton Park (Boleyn) ...	5 37	12 19	5 37	12 31	8 53	12 19
	Canning Town ...	5 37	11 15	5 37	11 12	8 53	11 7
	Royal Victoria Docks (Clyde Road) Morn.	5 37	8 14a.m.	5 39	8 10a.m.	—	—
	Even.	3 29p.m.	6 9p.m.	10 50	1 11Aft.	—	—
	Silvertown Station Morn.	6 9	8 8a.m.	6 9	8 10a.m.	—	—
	Even.	3 29	6 3	10 58	1 5Aft.	—	—
Leyton (Markhouse Road)	Walthamstow (Crooked Billet)	5 8	12 7	5 8	12 4	8 24	11 48
	Upton Park (Boleyn) ...	5 46	12 27	5 46	12 40	9 2	12 28
	Canning Town ...	5 46	11 23	5 46	11 21	9 2	11 16
	Royal Victoria Docks (Clyde Road) Morn.	5 46	8 23a.m.	5 46	8 19a.m.	—	—
	Even.	3 38p.m.	6 18p.m.	10 59	1 20Aft.	—	—
	Silvertown Station Morn.	6 18	8 17a.m.	6 18	8 19a.m.	—	—
	Even.	3 38	6 12	11 7	1 14Aft.	—	—
Thatched House	Walthamstow (Crooked Billet)	4 58	11 42	4 58	11 53	8 14	10 54
	Upton Park (Boleyn) ...	4 49*	12 37	4 49*	12 51	8 54*	12 38
	Canning Town ...	4 49*	11 33	4 49*	11 32	8 54*	11 26
	Royal Victoria Docks (Clyde Road) Morn.	4 49*	8 33a.m.	4 49*	8 29a.m.	—	—
	Even.	3 48p.m.	6 29p.m.	11 9	1 30Aft.	—	—
	Silvertown Station Morn.	6 28	8 27a.m.	6 28	8 29a.m.	—	—
	Even.	3 48	6 23	11 17	1 24Aft.	—	—
Wanstead Flats	Walthamstow (Crooked Billet)	4 52	11 36	4 52	11 47	8 8	10 48
	Leyton (Downsell Road) ...	4 35	11 52	4 35	11 47	8 8	11 48
	Upton Park (Boleyn) ...	4 55	12 43	4 55	12 51	9 0	12 44
	Canning Town ...	4 55	11 39	4 55	11 38	9 0	11 32
	Royal Victoria Docks (Clyde Road) Morn.	4 55	8 39a.m.	4 55	8 35a.m.	—	—
	Even.	3 54p.m.	6 35p.m.	11 15	1 36Aft.	—	—
	Silvertown Station Morn.	6 34	8 33a.m.	6 34	8 35a.m.	—	—
	Even.	3 54	6 29	11 23	1 30Aft.	—	—
Upton Park (Boleyn)	Walthamstow (Crooked Billet) ...	4 41	11 25	4 41	11 35	7 57	10 37
	Leyton (Downsell Road) ...	4 24	11 41	4 24	11 35	7 57	11 37
	Canning Town ...	5 6	11 50	5 6	11 50	9 12	11 43
	Royal Victoria Docks (Clyde Road) Morn.	5 6	8 50a.m.	5 6	8 48a.m.	—	—
	Even.	4 5p.m.	6 49p.m.	11 37	1 52Aft.	—	—
	Silvertown Station Morn.	6 46	8 45a.m.	6 46	8 47a.m.	—	—
	Even.	4 5	6 41	11 35	1 42Aft.	—	—
Canning Town	Walthamstow (Crooked Billet) ...	5 17	11 16	5 17	11 26	9 25	10 29
	Leyton (Downsell Road) ...	5 17	11 32	5 17	11 26	9 25	11 29
	Royal Victoria Docks (Clyde Road) Morn.	5 14	8 59a.m.	5 14	8 56a.m.	—	—
	Even.	4 14p.m.	6 58p.m.	11 24	2 0Aft.	—	—
	Silvertown Station Morn.	6 54	8 53	6 54	8 55	—	—
	Even.	4 14	6 50	11 29	1 50Aft.	—	—
Silvertown Station	Walthamstow (Crooked Billet) Morn.	7 11	9 9a.m.	7 11	9 9a.m.	—	—
	Even.	4 33	7 13	11 46	2 6Aft.	—	—

* From Leyton (Downsell Road) 3 minutes earlier.

SERVICE INTERVALS

BETWEEN	MONS.—FRIS. Peak (mins.)	MONS.—FRIS. Normal (mins.)	SATURDAYS Peak (mins.)	SATURDAYS Normal (mins.)	SUNDAYS Morn. (mins.)	SUNDAYS Aftn. (mins.)
Walthamstow (Crooked Billet) and Silvertown Stn.	6	—	6	—	—	—
Walthamstow (Crooked Billet and Canning Town) ...	6	6	6	8	8	8
Walthamstow (Crooked Billet) and Leyton (Markhouse Road)	3	6	3	4	8	4

ON PUBLIC HOLIDAYS trolleybuses run at special times which are advertised in the vehicles

★ GREEN LINE COACH GUIDE
TWOPENCE
From coach conductors or newsagents

ABBey 1234.

55

24th May, 1939
Waterlow & Sons Limited, London & Dunstable

Due to the elevated structure of Silvertown Way, many traction poles were placed in sockets. For much of its length, full-width bracket arms stretching across the road were positioned; as the wiring neared the Victoria Docks short-working at Clyde Road (shown here) conventional means were used. Just to the south is Clyde Road battery turn; movements were so frequent that eventually a wired turning circle was provided (in 1953). Long overdue, a trailing frog was cut into the northbound track, at pole 152 (with the request stop); the turn-out will be at pole 153 at the bracket arm. It is January 1938, just a few days before the 669 is projected from Canning Town to North Woolwich, the longest extension over roads previously unserved by trams. In the background is a bus on route 106; journeys to Clyde Road began on 3rd October 1934 shortly after the opening of Silvertown Way. These trips were withdrawn on 23rd July 1941 upon the introduction of trolleybus route 569. At the moment, only buses serve this point and even then only at irregular times. (London Transport Museum U26240)

Notice to— 33

Inspectors and Conductors, Walthamstow, West Ham and Poplar Depots. Workmen transfers through Canning Town Station—Routes 685 and 669.

Commencing on Monday, 9th February, 1948, Route 685 passengers at Workmen's Fares wishing to travel beyond Canning Town Station from points north thereof to points along Silvertown Way when service 685 operates to Canning Town Station only, will be allowed to transfer at the latter point to Route 669 trolleybuses.

Workmen's Tickets for these journeys will be punched in the direct journey section applicable, by Route 685 conductors and accepted on Route 669 without cancellation.

Workman Transfers— 385
Routes 669 and 685

Inspectors and conductors at Walthamstow, West Ham and Poplar Depots are notified that, commencing forthwith, passengers at workman fares to points between Silvertown Station and Woolwich Free Ferry will be allowed to transfer at all times at either Canning Town or Silvertown Stations, from Route 685 to Route 669.

Passengers at workman fares to Silvertown Station will also be allowed to transfer at Canning Town Station when Route 685 is curtailed at this point.

Pending the issue of tickets which are being reprinted to include these transfer facilities, tickets for these journeys must be punched in the direct journey section applicable by Route 685 conductors and accepted on Route 669 without cancellation.

This instruction cancels the existing instruction dated 15th September, 1948.

The photographer made a concerted effort to photograph the London trolleybus overhead – he considered it a bonus if he could get some vehicles in each view as well. He has achieved this at Clyde Road on 24th October 1959 where all four pieces of special equipment and two trolleybuses are seen. (John Gillham)

581 is working on route 669 to Stratford Broadway, a place it would have passed through many times in its career. Here, at Victoria Docks, the turning circle and siding can be seen; note the interesting span wire arrangement in the top foreground. (Don Thompson)

1398 lays over on Clyde Road turning circle on Saturday 5th October 1957; extended from the regular 685 terminus of Canning Town, workings such as this were provided to coincide with dockworkers' needs. It is 12.40pm so WH41, which is only going to GREEN STREET WEST HAM, will probably take on people finishing their five and a half day week. (Peter Mitchell)

398 is almost brand new and makes the battery manoeuvre at Clyde Road. At this time no overhead wires were provided and crews were not enamoured by all the trolley boom work required. 398 was destroyed by enemy action on Bexleyheath depot on 29th June 1944. (Charles Klapper)

Both the 669 and 685 had journeys turning at Victoria Docks; until 1953 an inspector, armed with a red lamp, oversaw movements at night time. No doubt there were times when trolleybuses turned without supervision but this was a risky exercise as a busy main road had to be crossed; E2 606 moves on battery at Clyde Road. Not everybody travelled by trolleybus – some extravagantly spent their hard-earned money on push bikes. (Charles Klapper)

During wartime a long queue of people are hoping to board one of two trolleybuses at Victoria Docks. Recently re-bodied 795A has just turned on battery power and is having its booms hoisted onto the overhead; it will soon gently manoeuvre past the waiting melee and pull up behind the vehicle in front. Those who are not successful in getting a place will not have to wait long as trolleybuses operate very frequently at peak times. Neither a route stencil, a running number or a side blind is exhibited – maybe 795A is an unscheduled EXTRA to Stratford Broadway. (London Transport Museum U19390)

The rundown shops are closed and Bob's café is not open on Sunday 3rd August 1952; L3 1398 is in North Woolwich Road, Silvertown. Many traction poles are located in railway property even the one supporting a feeder. Due to the location of the British Railways goods yard, traction poles beside it are on concrete islands on the very narrow kerb-line. The traction standard supporting the feeder on the other side of the road is located out of view way back in Barnwood Road, seen to the left of 1398. (Clarence Carter)

Silvertown flyover opened in 1934 with the bowstring bridge on Silvertown by-pass being a significant landmark in the area. E1 586 passes between the two arches while working on route 669 on 9th July 1959. (John Clarke)

The East End of London could look grim at times; the skyline looking towards exotic Silvertown says it all. E2 614 heads north for Stratford Broadway on route 669

The introduction of trolleybuses between Canning Town and North Woolwich was of great benefit as it eased the movement of those employed in the dock areas and at the Tate & Lyle sugar refinery. With Silvertown flyover in the background, three trolleybuses are in view; identifiable are 590 and 639 on the 669. It is 3rd August 1952. (Clarence Carter)

The grimy area of Silvertown is well illustrated by E2 625 working through to the Crooked Billet on route 685; it has just left the nearby short-working point. There are many items of interest: hoardings, a footbridge across Silvertown Station, a cobbled street and the Tate & Lyle sugar refinery. (Fred Ivey)

613 has dewired at the section insulator adjacent to Silvertown Station; the nearside boom is twisted and has been placed on a span wire – the offside one swings loosely. West Ham's breakdown wagon will attend and straighten the booms; it is Saturday 30th January 1960 so it is unlikely that 613 will need its services again as it will be withdrawn the following Tuesday. 613 is another to show CANNING TOWN VICTORIA DOCKS. Note the fairy lights adjacent to the running wires. (Tony Wright)

The entry and exit to Silvertown loop on 24th October 1959. This part of Albert Road featured a number of twin line hangers and interesting bridling arrangements at the points where the turning circle left and rejoined the main line. Traction poles positioned on railway property are used in the vicinity of the overhead junctions to enable bridling for the curves and special work to be anchored; further along the use of bracket arms is resumed. (John Gillham)

To cater for dockworkers, many journeys on route 685 went to Silvertown station where E1 591 turns from Albert Road into Leonard Street. On the left is traction standard number 12 on which are posted details of the imminent withdrawal of trolley-buses here. A few short-working points had their own pole number sequence – this was one of them. A number of parked cars impede 591's turn into Leonard Street. In the background is the railway line to North Woolwich. (Fred Ivey)

Trolleybuses traversing Silvertown loop used Leonard Street, Newland Street and Holt Road. E2 620 on the 669 turns from Leonard Street into Newland Street at 12.35 pm on Tuesday 29th September 1959, an unusual time to turn here. The conductor has changed the blind to show CANNING TOWN; it is assumed that there is no relieving crew for 620 at the top of Silvertown Way. (John Clarke)

E1 591 with M1 1532 behind, are in Newland Street where vehicles usually waited. It is January 1960 and time is almost up for 591 as it is due for withdrawal after service on 2nd February. (Fred Ivey)

1461 is in Holt Road – some drivers stood there as it gave them a better view of passing 669s; if they timed it correctly they would follow one as far as Canning Town – less passengers to pick up! A long journey lies ahead for 1461 as it is going to Crooked Billet. (Fred Ivey)

Road Power Services – Trolleybuses

Wednesday 27th July 1949
    12.17 p.m. Silvertown Substation Kempton Road Section
Faulty reclose relay caused C/B closing coil to burn out. Considerable
amount of smoke in Substation. Fire Brigade attended but did not
enter Substation.

                    8 mins.passenger delay
                   18 "   electrical delay

Rebodied 641C is parked in Holt Road one day in May 1952; it was one of nineteen vehicles returned to London, from Northern Coachbuilders, without seats – these were fitted on return to the capital. The new body lasted for a commendable thirteen years. E3C 641C is of course fitted with linen blinds; its next trip is to WANSTEAD FLATS on route 685. (John Clarke)

L3 1522 has just left Holt Road in the early afternoon of 5th December 1959; it is working one of the Saturday midday journeys that turned at Silvertown Station. It is another vehicle showing CANNING TOWN VICTORIA DOCKS though in this instance the 'display' is badly set; this is obviously a somewhat sloppy practice entertained at West Ham depot. Presumably, 1522's next two trips are working between these two points. (John Clarke)

This view was taken from a bridge over the railway that paralleled Albert Road for some distance; a road identified here is Auberon Street. E2 606 was always allocated to West Ham depot, so it worked on route 669 on a very regular basis. (Ken Blacker)

A short way further east in Albert Road, the yet-to-be commissioned overhead is officially photographed in January 1938. Traction poles utilise bowstring arms as they cannot be positioned on railway property due to the proximity of the tracks. (London Transport Museum U26237)

Near the Kent Arms public house, the road is flooded after a torrential downpour on 15th June 1948. E3 648 is marooned – maybe water has entered the electrical equipment, causing the vehicle to fail. The crew have abandoned 646 but have taken the precaution of dropping the booms. Children find 648 a play area in this run-down area of London. (London Transport Museum H16016)

619 is at the same place as the previous view with the conductor having already changed the front blind for its next trip to STRATFORD BROADWAY. This area suffered from wartime bombing; on the right some replacement pre-fabricated dwellings can be seen. The neglected buildings beyond the pre-fabs, seen earlier, have had a post-war makeover. (Phil Tatt)

Working on route 669, E2 628 is just west of the 'Prince Albert' and adjacent to the Odd Spot Café on 6th July 1959. Taken from a bridge over the railway the heavy cabling and infrastructure required for trolleybus operation is seen. The white band on the traction standard informs drivers that they are about to pass beneath a section breaker and should coast through. (Peter Mitchell)

1469 is on route 569 and passing the pre-fabs seen earlier. To the right is the North Woolwich signal box. A steam train stands in North Woolwich station; the signals and track are set against it. Sunblest advertise the virtues of their bread. (John Wills)

1447 is on route 569 and therefore works from Poplar depot. It has just turned from Pier Road into Albert Road on its way to Aldgate on 24th July 1959. It is a misapprehension that the 569 only operated in Monday to Saturday peaks – a few trips operated on Sunday mornings too. (Peter Mitchell)

A well-laden 613 turns from Pier Road into Albert Road; trolleybuses often clipped the kerb when doing this. It is Bank Holiday Monday, 3rd August 1959, so the shops are closed; later on there will be more people about. If they open, many will patronise the local fish and chip shop; others will visit the Royal Standard pub. (Mike Abbott)

Right outside the Prince Albert pub in May 1952, E2 604 turns from Albert Road into Pier Road. This vehicle spent virtually its whole working life on 'Docks services' (John Clarke)

To rid West Ham depot of its few remaining Leylands, a number of AEC J2 class vehicles were allocated in June 1954. One was 977 which is in Pier Road; it will soon reach North Woolwich terminus. In the background, a ship is having its cargo dealt with in King George V Dock. (Fred York)

Seen in Pier Road and by the station is 1482 which is PR 25 in the service. Route 569 was not introduced at the same time as the 565/567/665 in June 1940; it started in July 1941. (Fred Ivey)

J2 979 arrives at North Woolwich. It is an AEC that was moved from Walthamstow to West Ham depot in June 1954; this released the remaining P1 Leylands at West Ham. (Ron Wellings)

Soon after route 669 started, E2s 605 and 628 are at North Woolwich; 605's replacement offside panel appears to read RANSPORT rather than LONDON TRANSPORT. 605 is going the full length of the route to Stratford; 628 is only going to Canning Town where if it is to return south, may make a battery manoeuvre at the south end of Woodstock Street. (Charles Klapper)

L3 1456 and E2 622 have arrived at North Woolwich together; surprisingly the lower-powered 622 has caught up the higher-powered 1456. The pavement is not accessible at present and temporary wooden barriers force people to use the roadway; tubular metal frames positioned on wooden baulks channel them to safety. In the lower view, it seems that a telegraph pole helps to support the overhead; this is not so – the relevant traction poles are out of view. With 1456 moving off, a low-standing 'ALIGHTING POINT ONLY' bus stop flag is revealed. (David Savage)

643C is on the 669; it uses the original destination blind description for Stratford Broadway. By looking at other 669 photos, readers will note that via points were later dispensed with for this display.

Route 685 in its extremity was a very long route – Crooked Billet to North Woolwich. Few journeys operated over the entire length – most North Woolwich trips only went to FINDEN ROAD GREEN STREET or GREEN STREET WEST HAM. E2 602C exemplifies the latter description. To the right, a pontoon leads to the free ferry. (Lyndon Rowe)

On 27th November 1951, Lea Bridge's 1354 is a long way from its normal stomping grounds. Usually to be seen on Lea Bridge Road and through Hackney and onto Bloomsbury, it is on training duties at North Woolwich. One reason for the instructor taking the novice down here was the possibility of the new man being loaned to West Ham and needing to be familiarised with the overhead. Another explanation is that the three mile stretch from Canning Town to North Woolwich was ideal for trainee drivers; with only two intermediate turning circles and few road junctions, a novice was able to concentrate on vehicle handling and section insulators. (Alan Cross)

London Transport arranged for some of the wiring between Canning Town and North Woolwich to be photographed before the introduction of route 669; a neat symmetrical circle was erected with few span wires used inside it. A Leyland Titan TD and an STL wait to depart on route 101. In the background is the entrance to the foot tunnel beneath the River Thames – many preferred to use this means of getting to Woolwich as opposed to waiting for the ferry. (London Transport Museum U26236)

Loading up and ready for departure is E2 609 which is outside the rotunda here and at the start of an inevitably busy journey to Stratford Broadway. 609 shows items that will disappear with the onset of war. Gone will be the original deep rear mudguards, the advertisements adjacent to the rear indicator boxes and the offside route stencil. (Charles Klapper)

Most Weymann rebodied trolleybuses were allocated to West Ham depot on their return to London. With their new bodies, drivers changed the front destination blind as opposed to the conductor who had carried out this task hitherto. 406A would later see service at Hanwell and Bexleyheath depots. At North Woolwich, it is accompanied by Poplar's 1488 on route 569. (Ronald Bristow)

North Woolwich was one of a number of termini where it would have been useful to have had an overtaking loop; with no such facility available, this meant that sometimes poles were dropped; L3 1520 overtakes N2 1669 on 18th September 1959. Note that 1669 has 669 as its route and registration number. (Ron Wellings)

CANNING TOWN TO POPLAR DEPOT

1533 on route 665 passes straight through the main Canning Town junction; 603 on the 685 will follow it for a few more yards and then turn left into Silvertown Way on its way to Victoria Docks. To be in alignment with Poplar's trolleybuses, West Ham used their higher–powered vehicles on the 567s/665s – with the withdrawal of these routes in November 1959, the M1s found themselves working on other services. (Fred Ivey)

1470 passes through Canning Town on its way to Aldgate. There seems to be an extraordinary amount of span wire here but it was all needed to keep the junction safely aloft. Even in the late 1950s the 'advert boys' had their slogans; a hoarding encourages men to enjoy a 'Double Diamond Daily'.

1515 on route 569 turns from East India Dock Road into Silvertown Way. At stage four of the conversion programme, 1515 moved to Finchley depot – at stage twelve it was transferred to Fulwell and was in service on a date that London trolleybuses would rather forget – 8th May 1962. (Fred Ivey)

567

569
MON. - FRI.
RUSH HOURS

665
FARE STAGE

ON AND AFTER JUNE 9

Route 565 - Weekday peak hours
EAST HAM TOWN HALL & HOLBORN

Route 665 - - - Daily
BARKING & BLOOMSBURY
Additional service - Sundays
POPLAR AND SMITHFIELD

Route 567 - Weekdays only
BARKING RD GREEN STREET & ALDGATE
Extended to Barking Saturday afternoons and evenings

TIMES OF FIRST AND LAST TROLLEYBUSES

POINTS	MONDAY to FRIDAY		SATURDAY		SUNDAY	
	First Morn.	Last Night	First Morn.	Last Night	First Morn.	Last Night
Barking (New London Road) to						
Aldgate	{ 4 16 / 4 58	11 30	{ 4 16 / 4 58	{ 12 10 / 1 44	...	...
Bloomsbury	5 17	11 10	5 17	11 43	6 33	11 18
Canning Town	{ 4 16 / 4 58	12 30	{ 4 16 / 4 58	{ 12 27 / 1 44	6 33	12 34
Greengate Street	{ 4 16 / 4 58	{ 12 43 / 1 39	{ 4 16 / 4 58	{ 12 32 / 1 44	6 33	12 34
East Ham Town Hall to						
Aldgate	4 21	11 35	4 21	{ 12 15 / 1 49	...	...
Bloomsbury	5 7	11 15	5 7	11 48	6 38	11 23
Holborn	6 47	6 29	6 47	1 21Aft.	...	...
Canning Town	4 21	12 47	4 21	{ 12 32 / 1 49	6 38	12 39
Greengate Street	4 21	{ 12 48 / 1 44	4 21	{ 12 37 / 1 49	6 38	12 39
Barking	{ 4 7 / 4 48	{ 12 30 / 1 26	4 7	{ 12 15 / 1 34	6 21	12 21
Green Street (Barking Road) to						
Aldgate	4 25	11 39	4 25	{ 12 19 / 1 53	...	...
Bloomsbury	4 38	11 19	4 38	11 52	6 42	11 27
Holborn	6 51	6 33	6 51	1 25Aft.	...	...
Canning Town	4 25	12 52	4 25	{ 12 55 / 1 53	6 42	12 45
Barking	{ 4 3 / 4 44	{ 12 26 / 1 22	4 3	{ 12 11 / 1 30	6 17	12 17
Canning Town to						
Aldgate	4 34	11 49	4 34	{ 12 29 / 2 3	...	...
Bloomsbury	4 23	11 29	4 23	12 2	{ 6 13 / 6 51	11 37
Holborn	6 22	6 43	6 22	1 35Aft.	...	...
Green Street	*3 54	{ 12 42 / 1 12	*3 54	1 20	6 8	12 49
Barking	{ *3 54 / *4 51	{ 12 16 / 1 12	{ *3 54 / *4 51	{ 12 1 / 1 20	6 8	12 7
Blackwall Tunnel to						
Aldgate	4 38	11 53	4 38	{ 12 33 / 2 7	...	...
Bloomsbury	4 27	11 33	4 27	12 6	4 48	11 41
Smithfield	...	...	...	...	9 33	9 25
Holborn	6 26	6 47	6 26	1 39Aft.	...	...
Green Street	5 15	12 38	5 15	1 16	6 12	12 45
Canning Town	5 15	12 17	5 15	1 22	5 59	12 45
Barking	5 15	12 12	5 15	{ 11 57 / 1 16	6 12	12 3
Aldgate to						
Green Street	†4 57	{ 7 32 / 12 18	4 57	12 56	...	...
Blackwall Tunnel	†4 57	12 18	4 57	12 56	...	...
Barking	...	...	4 57	{ 11 34 / 12 56		
Bloomsbury to						
Blackwall Tunnel	5 3	12 13	5 3	12 46	5 27	12 21
Canning Town	5 3	12 1	5 3	12 46	5 27	12 9
Greengate Street	5 3	11 56	5 3	12 46	5 40	12 9
Barking	5 3	11 36	5 3	11 21	5 40	11 27
Holborn (Grays Inn Road) to						
East Ham	6 58	7 22	6 58	2 14Aft.	...	...
Smithfield to						
Poplar	...	...	...	...	10 3	9 57

† To Barking.   * From Poplar Depot 8 minutes earlier.

SERVICE INTERVALS

BETWEEN	MONDAY to FRIDAY		SATURDAY		SUNDAY	
	Peak Mins.	Normal Mins.	Peak Mins.	Normal Mins.	Morn. Mins.	Aftn. Mins.
East Ham Town Hall and Holborn	2	—	2	—	5	3–4
Barking and Bloomsbury	3	3–4	3	3–4	5	4
Poplar and Smithfield	—	—	—	—	5	—
Barking Road (Green St.) and Aldgate	4–6	6	—	4‡	—	—
Poplar and Aldgate	2	2–4	3	3–4	—	—
Barking and Aldgate	—	—	—	4‡	—	—

‡ Afternoons and Evenings only.

40—5056D—450/2 ch.

Waterlow & Sons Limited, London & Dunstable.

At the East India Dock Road/Silvertown Way junction, 1389 heads for West Ham depot. Overhead leading to the left is used solely by route 569; the frog is set for the 'straight'. In the absence of a pointsman and electric re-set skate, it is an uncommon example of a 'pull and hold down' frog for a right turn. (Fred Ivey)

1484 at the Bridge House pub at Canning Town on 3rd October 1959 is running into Poplar depot on route 665; it is very smart and a credit to their cleaning staff. Passengers wishing to travel further west will need to board either a bus or trolleybus to take them to their destinations. (L. Nicholson, courtesy Transport Treasury)

```
Traffic Delay - Wednesday, the 6th August, 1952 -
Trolleybus Services - Canning Town Area.


        At 11.35 p.m. on the above date, there was a delay
of 20 minutes to the trolleybus services in the Canning
Town area, caused by the breakdown of the London Electricity
Board's high tension supply to Canning Town Substation,
due, it is understood, to severe storm.
```

Between July and September 1957, nineteen D class trolleybuses were sold to George Cohen & Sons and broken up at their premises in Bidder Street, Canning Town; this was strictly a no-go area to the public. In the first picture a couple of Ds are seen at the entrance of the yard awaiting scrapping. In the second and third views, 531's body is lifted into an area where its remains will be dealt with – a sad end to a trolleybus that worked its whole life at Hammersmith depot. London Transport did not generally separate body from chassis but somehow Cohen's have achieved this. (Fred Ivey)

A funeral pyre at Cohen's Canning Town yard has played havoc with this metal body shell; however, even from the twisted remains it can be discerned that this was once 384, the only D1 class vehicle in the fleet and the only Leyland to carry rear wheel spats. Cohen's main interest in the bodywork was to salvage as much aluminium as possible resulting in all external panels being removed before the remains were burnt. (Ron Lunn)

On rainy days, traffic tends to be slow and is probably the reason for 1654 running late – to get it back on time for its next trip it has been curtailed at Arbour Square.1654 passes over the Iron Bridge at Canning Town. It is allocated to West Ham depot; it will be observed that the destination display for Arbour Square differed to the one used by Poplar's trolleybuses (see page 155). (Michael Dryhurst)

Mr Dryhurst was a determined individual when it came to photographing London trolleybuses – he was not deterred by rain. A few yards west, he has captured 1463 working only as far as TRINITY CHURCH CANNING TOWN on route 567. (Michael Dryhurst)

Part of the 665 service only went as far as Clerkenwell Green. This is shown by 1451 which has just passed the facing frog at the junction of East India Dock Road and Abbott Road. (Fred Ivey)

Between June 1940 and January 1949, movements for trolleybuses short-working at Poplar was clockwise via Aberfeldy Street, Blair Street and Benledi Street; these were Sunday 567s and 665 'nighters'. In 1949, the line of travel altered and vehicles turned anti-clockwise – via Abbott Road, Blair Street and Aberfeldy Street. Until May 1958, through services used East India Dock Road in both directions; that year London Transport embarked upon a second major rewiring pro-gramme in the east end of London (the other was at Ilford) – this was due to a new northern approach to the Blackwall Tunnel being constructed. Eastbound trolleybuses were diverted away from East India Dock Road and travelled via St Leonard's Road, Hilditch Street, a temporary un-named road and Drew Street before continuing along Blair Street (which became clockwise again) and Abbott Road to regain line of route in East India Dock Road. Changes were also made for vehicles entering and leaving Poplar depot; a downside of the alterations was that the facility to turn from the east was lost.

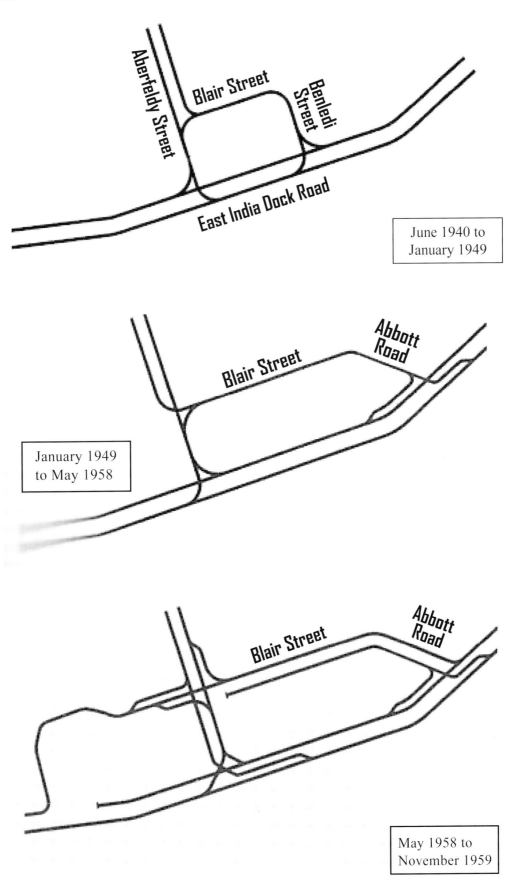

121

This is the junction of Abbott Road (to the left) with East India Dock Road on 17th October 1959; the photographer faces east and has simultaneously captured a northbound and southbound trolleybus. Wires to the left had been used by trolleybuses accessing Poplar depot from the west; with the diversion now in operation they, along with the 'through' eastbound wires, and the right turn wires from East India Dock Road into Abbott Road, are redundant but remain live. (John Gillham)

On 15th January 1933 the alignment of East India Dock Road was changed and improved at a point near Abbott Road. A new bridge over both Bow Creek (River Lea) and the railway at Canning Town Station was built with a more direct course than hitherto being adopted – originally the roadway with the tramway had crossed the river with a short right and left turn. The boundary between the County of London and West Ham Corporation was in the middle of the river but the plough change pit where eastbound trams changed to the overhead and westbound trams to the conduit power pick-up was at the foot of the bridge approach on the Poplar side. The original conduit pit became disused and a new one constructed on the new alignment (this may have been the last new change pit constructed on London's streets). With the abandonment of trams after operation on 8th June 1940, the new pit was removed; however, the old one and disused roadway remained in-situ and outlived the replacement trolleybuses. Looking east, 1467 is the first of two L3s heading westwards and are on the revised alignment of East India Dock Road; the frog giving access to Abbott Road and Poplar depot can be seen. Note former tram standards still in position in the change pit area. (Roy Hubble)

Former West Ham Corporation tram 334 pauses at the new change pit; the single trolley arm has been run round the car and placed under the retaining hook in preparation for its next eastbound trip. At present it is working on route 67 to Aldgate. 334 was sent to Hampstead depot with the conversion of the Barking Road/Commercial routes in June 1940. Late in the war it was fitted with windscreens and sent to south London where it managed to stay operational until the last day that trams ran in London – 5th July 1952 (D.W.K. Jones)

Many RT and RTL motorbuses were held in store between 1954 and 1958; one was RTL 1600 which was allocated to Athol Street Garage in February 1958. Not only did work on the approach to the Blackwall tunnel affect trolleybus services, it also impinged on routes 108 and 108A which were diverted in both directions. Southbound, this involved using Blair Street and Abbott Road where a right hand turn was made into East India Dock Road; three minutes extra running time was allowed for this. RTL 1600 heads for ELTHAM SOUTHEND CRESCENT. The front dome is dented, indicating that the roof has clipped either a tree or the tunnel wall. To the left can be seen the facing and trailing frog of what had been trolleybus access to Poplar depot from the west. (Fred Ivey)

The photographer is in Aberfeldy Street on 17th October 1959; 1464 heads west along East India Dock Road – chimneys and cranes are typical of dock areas. Fourteen traction poles adjacent to the boundary wall of the East India Dock had anti-climb guards fitted – these spiked metal collars were positioned to prevent people gaining access to the dock. The eastbound wiring between Blackwall Tunnel and Abbott Road could have been removed after May 1958; because an electric feeder for the area was situated east of this junction, this could not take place. (John Gillham)

With the revised access arrangement to Poplar depot having been in force for some time, 1446 moves from East India Dock Road into Aberfeldy Street on 12th March 1959. L3 1446 follows a stablemate down Aberfeldy Street towards the depot. (David Clarke)

Between January 1949 and May 1958, trolleybuses entering Poplar depot from the east used Abbott Road, Blair Street and Aberfeldy Street. With the new arrangements they travelled along East India Dock Road to turn right into Aberfeldy Street via a new frog (reverting to the original way of accessing the depot from the east). 1474 moves from East India Dock Road into Aberfeldy Street.

From January 1949, trolleybuses taking up service from Poplar depot and heading west travelled the length of Aberfeldy Street before turning right into East India Dock Road; 1476 performs this manoeuvre; the driver needs to change the destination blind. In the background, the new Lansbury estate has replaced slum areas.

1446 is parked on the cobbles in Aberfeldy Street. The lack of traffic indicates a Sunday when much of the daytime 567 service operated between Poplar and Aldgate. For its last eighteen months of trolleybus operation Aberfeldy Street was wired both ways.

It is the last days of Poplar depot's trams and E1 848 is in Aberfeldy Street on the single line track that leads to the depot. Withdrawn in June 1940, it was stored in Hampstead depot in case it needed to be reinstated as a replacement for a damaged car; this did not occur and it was scrapped in the early post-war period – some of its stable mates were more fortunate and, fitted with windscreens, survived into the 1950s. This is the original trolleybus overhead layout here with the right turn being used by the all night service and short-working trolleybuses from the west. (London Transport Museum U31496)

1481 takes up service from Poplar depot and turns from Aberfeldy Street into Blair Street. Saturday 7th November 1959 was a murky day so the driver has switched the side and interior lights on. Temporary traffic signals pertain. (Jack Gready)

Looking north, on 17th October 1959, this is the new trolleybus junction installed at Aberfeldy Street in 1958. L3 1436 has negotiated it on its way to Poplar depot. (John Gillham)

1518, running into Poplar depot, is at the north end of Aberfeldy Street and about to cross Abbott Road. A Metropolitan police sign states that only trolleybuses are allowed to travel south down Aberfeldy Street. Despite this, RTL1091 on route 108 is on diversion on its trip to Bromley-by-Bow.

A different sign has been installed in exactly the same place as the one in the previous view – maybe somebody has acquired it as a treasured piece of street furniture! A sign such as this would be worth a fortune today. Spelt wrongly, TROLLEY BUSES will not fit into one line (Sid Hagarty)

With Poplar depot in the background, 1485 is in an un-named road and about to cross Abbott Road to enter Aberfeldy Street. The driver shows the correct display of COMMERCIAL RD ALDGATE; if he had used the regular Aldgate display it would have shown a via point through which it would not have passed – CANNING TOWN. (Peter Moore)

On British soil for virtually the last time, 1868 is towed away from Poplar garage by service vehicle 401W. A new life will find it in San Sebastian where it will become number 84 in their fleet. (Fred Ivey)

Poplar depot and its surroundings were recipients of German bombs in October 1940 – the desolate area in the foreground was once houses. Unfortunate though that was, it has allowed an almost full view of the façade of the depot to be seen nineteen years later on 17th October 1959 – the portals are distinctive LCC design. (John Gillham)

Poplar depot still exists though the portals are bricked up; it is occupied by 'Iron Mountain' who specialise in shredding paper. The building was so well built that if it ever needs to be demolished (and Hitler couldn't do it) it will take some weeks. Entering Poplar depot on 17th October 1959 is L3 1481. (John Gillham)

1440 leaves Poplar depot, on 26th September 1959, as an EXTRA to Barking; a crew has been found to work some overtime. Their devotion to duty will enable supporters to get to a football match at West Ham United's ground a bit quicker. (Ron Wellings)

It is 15th May 1940 and a large number of new trolleybuses have been delivered to Poplar depot before the tram to trolleybus conversion date of 9th June 1940; all vehicles here are L3s. Maybe Dunlop had the contract for adverts on the rear of all trolleybuses initially allocated here; presumably all are fitted with their tyres so maybe there is a deal between them and London Transport. For the welfare of the staff, radiators have been fitted to the depot wall. (London Transport Museum U31455)

21st August 1957, and in exactly the same place seventeen years after the previous photograph was taken; Poplar was only ever allocated L3s and three are seen in this view. OXO and A55 Austin Cars are advertised on the rear of 1430 and 1447. Until the change of direction in Blair Street in the late 1940s, trolleybuses running into Poplar depot showed POPLAR ABERFELDY STREET. After that, POPLAR ABBOTT ROAD was displayed as the last alighting point for vehicles running into the depot. (London Transport Museum NH1406)

A number of L3s, headed by 1508 are seen, poles up in Poplar depot. Although everything looks serene, a fuelling island ominously indicates that trolleybuses will not be here much longer and that motorbuses will soon replace them. (Don Thompson)

At the time this photograph was taken of 1464 over the pits in Poplar depot, no-one would have known that this vehicle would be the last service trolleybus to enter it – in the first few minutes of Wednesday 11th November 1959. Maintenance was an important aspect of trolleybus operation and the checking of tyres, bodywork, electrical and mechanical equipment was carried out regularly.

Due to the large amount of spare space in Poplar depot, withdrawn buses were stored there during the 1950s: STLs and Ts were to be found. In the first view, STLs form a backdrop to a very forlorn 640 which will soon make a one-way trip to Bird's scrapyard at Stratford upon Avon. In the second picture, a couple of 14T12 buses accompany 1491 which is seen 'poles down'. (John L. Smith)

Upon withdrawal, a number of SAs were parked in Poplar depot (August to November 1959). 1727 and 1744 are placed in an area where there are no overhead wires so they have been manhandled into position as they are not fitted with traction batteries. Also in view are a number of L3s; 1520 is one and although its trolley arms may stretch to the troughing, the next driver may opt to use battery mode to get beneath them. By this time six stabling tracks have been removed from this part of the shed. (Fred Ivey)

Poplar garage was used in 1961 to store 125 Q1 class trolleybuses before they were shipped to Spain. 1788 is parked alongside RM 133 which has been operating on trolleybus replacement route 5A. All the overhead wiring was removed a long time ago (Fred Ivey)

Back where Abbott Road met East India Dock Road (see page 120). 1486 heads east on 1st January 1959 which then was an ordinary working day; it had been on route 569 earlier on but is now making a miscellaneous eastbound movement. A service driver is in the cab so maybe he is taking it to West Ham depot for some reason. On the left, an RTL is on the 106. The westbound overhead in Blair Street is now disused. (John Clarke)

On 4th October 1959, Poplar's 1475 is in Blair Street working east on route 665; the wires in the other direction have been redundant since May 1958 – no attempt was ever made to remove them. The conductor is using a ticket punch and rack just as he/she had done since taking up employment in this role. It is the last day that this will occur as fare collection duties will involve the use of a Gibson ticket issuing machine on the following day at both Poplar and West Ham depots. In fact this will complete the change from Punch and Rack to Gibson machine on the entire London Transport network. (Lyndon Rowe)

1439 is in Blair Street and about to turn right into Aberfeldy Street for Poplar depot. Route 565 was only ever a weekday rush hour service – by the time it was withdrawn in 1956 it only worked on Mondays to Fridays. With 565s/569s only working in rush hours it meant that 567s/665s carried all the passengers between Canning Town and Gardiners Corner outside peak times. (David Chapman)

Removal of trees, Blair Street.

6.   Because of damage caused to passing trolleybuses, it has been necessary to remove some of the trees in Blair Street. We have considered the possibility of replacing the trees with a smaller variety but in view of the recent experience of wanton damage to young trees planted in the Borough we have decided to leave this matter in abeyance for the time being.

This is an interim layout at the Aberfeldy Street/Blair Street/ Drew Street junction; trolleybuses from the east and west accessing Poplar depot still use Blair Street westbound along which 1469 is traversing. Without a large number of vehicles heading east along Blair Street and the police signal lights not in use, the diversionary route has not yet been implemented. Before it does, the wiring under which 1469 is travelling will be tied off here; then trolleybuses leaving Poplar depot and heading east will turn left from Aberfeldy Street into Blair Street. If, and it is if, the facing frog at the top of Aberfeldy Street allows it, trolleybuses will still be able to turn left into East India Dock Road. (Fred Ivey)

A few yards further on, 1469 is in difficulties as it moves from Blair Street into Aberfeldy Street; the revised overhead layout is in transition and in theory, Blair Street can be used in both directions. It would take some time for drivers to learn the new overhead configurations here; it looks as if 1469 has got stuck on 'the dead' – once the shenanigans of trolley boom manipulation are over, 1462 will follow it into Poplar depot. (Fred Ivey)

On the afternoon of 4th November 1959, L3 1451 moves from Drew Street into Aberfeldy Street. Presumably there is no relieving crew so 1451 will be parked in Aberfeldy Street until taken up later on. Two policemen can be seen – one in white, one in black. (John Clarke)

In 1959, depot code plates started to disappear from London Transport vehicles; being detachable they were easily removed as souvenirs. Without one, L3 1441 is PR 29 on route 567 and turns from Drew Street into Aberfeldy Street; in a few minutes it will reach Poplar depot to be spun round on the turntable/traverser and positioned for its next trip. The driver could have made a better job of showing POPLAR ABBOTT ROAD as part of the previous display (SILVERTOWN STATION) can be seen.

1491 heading east, passes through the multi-way junction erected where Aberfeldy Street met Drew Street and Blair Street. Traffic competes for road space; heading it is a motorbike and a sidecar – its driver has no crash helmet. Of interest is the turn-out erected to enable Sunday 567s and night 665s to turn back to London; extraordinarily, a wood backed frog (rare for this part of London at the time) is used. The frog under which 1491's trolley heads are passing is operated by a handle on the traction pole seen in the right foreground of the next picture. The frog pulley wire is almost at the top of that traction standard; a sleeve above the overhead track allows its purpose to be fulfilled.

It is 10th November 1959, the last day of the 567 trolleybus. 1436 is in Hilditch Street with a British Road Services vehicle as company. Although typical housing of the area and era can be seen, much demolition has taken place in the vicinity to accommodate the new Blackwall tunnel approach. The wiring was erected by London Transport linesmen – presumably the expenditure was reclaimed from the local authority. A special pole sequence (1–17) was created for the diversion. (Brian Speller)

All eastbound traffic was diverted away from East India Dock Road. L3 1441, a 665 to Barking, is in the un-named road on 1st January 1959 – bosom buddy is RTL 723 is on the 40. A close-up view of 1441 shows the desolation better. (John Clarke)

The changes to the overhead at Poplar were probably incorporated in blanket powers; new routeings for trolleybuses normally needed formal approval. Seen in Hilditch Street, L3 1431 heads for Barking; in the background, work on the new northern approach to the Blackwall tunnel is well advanced.

1654's destination is West Ham depot; it is in St Leonard's Road showing **WEST HAM GREENGATE ST**. There was no facility on the farechart for passengers to be carried between 'Greengate' and the depot.

1496 turns into St Leonard's Road. Connoisseurs could tell a Poplar and West Ham trolleybus apart; WH showed **BARKING BDY** while PR displayed **BARKING**. The demolition needed in association with the roadworks is reminiscent of war damage the area suffered fifteen years previously. (John Wills)

The compiler of the following books details amendments to them

TROLLEYBUSES IN WEST LONDON

Page 26. Lower photo. This is at the junction of Penrhyn Road and St James's Road.

Page 74. Top photo. The ampersands were not omitted from the Hounslow depot blinds – they were painted out.

Page 103. Bottom photo. The blind display of the second vehicle is correct – there is a VIA in front of HANWELL.

Page 122. Top photo. The bubble-car stated was cut out by the printer.

TROLLEYBUSES IN NORTH-WEST LONDON

Page 120. Middle photo was taken near the bottom of Barnet Hill and not New Barnet.

TROLLEYBUSES IN OUTER NORTH LONDON

Page 57. Lower photo. 1511 has turned at Wood Green from the south, not as stated.

TROLLEYBUSES IN NORTH-EAST LONDON

Frontispiece. The second vehicle mentioned in the caption was cut out by the printer.

Page 3. 1345 is heading south – the destination blind has not been changed.

Page 74. Bottom photo. 1251 is just west of Bell Junction.

Page 92. Top photo. Billet Road should read Blackhorse Road.

Page 106. Top photo. 629C is closer to Walthamstow depot than Crooked Billet.

Page 108. Top photo should be attributed to Michael Dryhurst.

TROLLEYBUSES IN EAST LONDON

Page 3. Introduction. Third paragraph did not state the termini of route 665 – these were Barking and Bloomsbury.

Page 15. This is trolleybus 335 not 336.

Page 63. Bottom two photos are at Barking not Chadwell Heath.

Page 115. Bottom photo is in Plashett Road, not Plashett Grove.

Page 124. The correction sheet is for North East London not East London; also should state for page 74 that 1251 is west of Bell Junction.

Page 127. Ls should read L3 in photo caption.

While work on the new approach to the Blackwall tunnel continues, 1502 passes by. Most wiring alterations took place in the small hours – the two night 665s turning at Poplar would either have been towed through by service vehicle or passed by on battery. (Jack Gready)

With the original entrance to the Blackwall Tunnel to the right 1484 is a 567 to Aldgate. 1484 moved from Poplar to Finchley in 1959, it ended its days at Stonebridge depot. The big structure behind the trolleybus is the main gateway to the old East India Dock. (Fred Ivey)

On 1st January 1959, L3 1432 heads for Aldgate while working on route 567. Work is progressing steadily on the new northern approach to the Blackwall tunnel; the original eastbound wiring has long been removed. (John Clarke)

POPLAR TO LIMEHOUSE

Trolleybuses still travel normally along East India Dock Road; not for much longer though for those travelling east will soon be diverted – newly strung overhead leads into St Leonard's Road. Poplar's 1461 on the 569 and West Ham's 1560 on the 665 pass under a section feeder. (Fred Ivey)

The new arrangements are in force and trolleybuses now turn from East India Dock Road into St Leonard's Road. The feeder has been transferred to the new wires. This photograph was taken on 17th October 1959. (John Gillham)

A short way west from the Blackwall Tunnel, 1469 heads for Bloomsbury on 15th March 1958. At the moment, traffic can freely pass both ways in East India Dock Road; two months later a one-way system will be introduced locally and will pertain for the rest of the trolleybus era. (Bus of Yesteryear)

Many trolleybuses on routes 567 and 665 only went as far as East Ham Town Hall; exemplifying this on 26th September 1959 is L3 1463. In the background is George Green's School. (Ron Wellings)

On 6th July 1959 L3 1464 is by Hale Street while working on route 567 to Aldgate. Before long it will be at Finchley depot where on 7th November 1961 it will be the last trolleybus to operate around the Holborn Loop. It was transferred to Fulwell in January 1962 and worked there until the last day of London's trolleybuses (Peter Mitchell)

At Annabel Close, Poplar L3 1434 is EX2: Poplar is running EXTRAs for a football match at West Ham on Saturday 7th November 1959. It will be the last time that this happens as Poplar will be finishing with trolleybuses in three days time. (Lyndon Rowe)

West Ham's 1532 is outside the LCC Centre on 6th July 1959 heading for Aldgate on the 567; at various times the route was ex-tended to Smithfield. The 567 will feature in stage four of the trolleybus conversion programme: 1532 will be ominously involved at stage six – withdrawal. (Peter Mitchell)

L3 1481 is at Stainsby Road at 6.39pm on 24th July 1959; it is working on route 569 but only going to ARBOUR SQUARE COMMERCIAL RD. Trolleybuses working on the Commercial Road routes were subject to traffic delays so curtailments were frequent (Peter Mitchell)

MILE END TO WEST INDIA DOCKS

Crossing Mile End Road on 28th March 1959, K2 1259 passes from Grove Road into Burdett Road. In earlier years, there was an un-frogged connection from Mile End Road into Burdett Road which was one of a number not used for any service requirements; it was removed in early 1950. (John Gillham)

1143 passes the end of Timothy Road, the exit point for Burdett Road loop on 14th March 1959; it was one of a number of facilities rarely used so the facing frog into Baggally Street was removed in December 1949. However, trolleybuses could still turn there if necessary with power being obtained via the trailing frog. The request stop in view is used by route 106 which travelled via Timothy Road and St Pauls Way; this detour avoided passing beneath Burdett Road bridge that was safely passed by trams and trolleybuses – an anomaly as trolleybuses were taller than motorbuses. (John Clarke)

Re-vamped tram 1260 passes beneath Burdett Road bridge while working on route 77 to WEST INDIA DK. It is the last days of this service as trolleybus wires can clearly be seen under the arched bridge. (D. W. K. Jones)

Passing under Burdett Road Bridge on 12th March 1959, K2 1250 heads north. With Smithfield meat market closed on Sundays, half the service on route 677 only operated between West India Docks and Mildmay Park. (David Clarke)

1245 pauses on its north-bound 677 trip to allow 1142 to pass under Burdett Road bridge on 14th March 1959. Burdett Road station was situated on the top of the bridge until 1941 when a minor bombing incident occurred; the buildings were patched up and the station reopened. However a second and more serious incident occurred the following year which saw the station close for good. The turning loop at Timothy Road, some way north, was described as BURDETT ROAD STATION when Charlton Works made blinds. With the station closed BURDETT ROAD was displayed on blinds made at Aldenham. (John Clarke)

On 21st April 1956, K2 1287 passes beneath the bridge while working south; simultaneously, a passenger steam-hauled train passes overhead. 1287 passed to Wood Green depot when Clapton finished with it – stage two – and would remain in service there until stage twelve. Even then it was held in store at Fulwell as a Rolling Stock Engineer's spare vehicle in case, as a Leyland, it needed to be returned to service at Isleworth. This did not occur but it was not passed to Mr George Cohen until 14th April 1962. At the time this photograph was taken 1287 has almost another six years to stay in one piece! (Peter Mitchell)

K2 1307 has just passed the Burdett Road/Commercial Road/West India Dock overhead complex while working on route 677 to Smithfield on 14th March 1959. Heading south, a couple of lorries are given priority by the on-duty policeman. (John Clarke)

IT is now 20 years since the old tramlines were taken up on the route from Smithfield to the West India Docks and replaced by trolleybuses. The operation was completed just in time, for the old tram service would have been far more vulnerable to the road craters caused by bombs than the trolleybuses ever were.

Now the day of the trolleybuses on the 677 route is over, and this familiar sight of a 677 trolleybus passing the Eastern Hotel by the West India Dock Road, will be seen no more.

On Tuesday the last trolleybuses covered the route. On Wednesday morning the new 277 diesel buses replaced them, and extended their journey to Cubitt Town by way of West Ferry Road.

This extension has been greatly welcomed by people living on the Isle of Dogs.

Mr. Crane, the Cubitt Town newsagent, said "People going to work in the rush hour seem delighted with the extra buses. The only complaint of local residents is that the last one of the day is still too early to help Island people who have gone to the cinema or the theatre and arrive home late."

Halifax Photos.

144

Just turning into West India Dock Road, K1A 1123A is less than a mile away from the southern terminus of route 677. Only two Weymann rebodied vehicles lasted until the start of the conversion programme – one was 1123A which was withdrawn at stage two (the other one was 1587A). (Norman Rayfield)

On 14th March 1959, K1 1259 has just entered West India Dock Road and is about to pass beneath the trailing frog which connects trolleybus routes from the Commercial Road. With the lack of advertisers in the late 1950s, a number of vehicles (including 1259) were fitted with 'stock bills'. (John Clarke)

1259 is at the western end of West India Dock Road; it has just passed through the facing frog which takes the 677 north, and Commercial Road routes west. It is 11th April 1959 and soon the two items of overhead special equipment seen here will be removed. (Jack Gready)

1445 is in West India Dock Road working on the peak hour leg of route 567 to West India Docks. Latterly this section operated to a fifteen minute headway during peak times. (Stuart Johnson)

E1 trams 901 and 1147 are parked near the West India Docks terminus of tram route 77; another is on the stub by the railway bridge. 901s next trip will only be as far as SOUTHGATE RD. (W. A. Camwell)

E1 tram 599 is at the West India Dock terminus of route 77 in 1937; it is an open-fronted car which will receive windscreens in due course. The 77 ran between West India Docks and Aldersgate; with no suitable facilities for turning trolleybuses there, the replacing 677 was diverted to Smithfield. Here, the conductor has the benefit of a metal hood over the tram wire so he can easily position the trolley arm.

1123A turns into Ming Street, being just a minute or so away from West India Docks terminus. The driver has already changed his blind for the return trip to Smithfield; in the background an RTL on route 56 can be observed. Note the ornate lamp standard. It is 14th March 1959 and exactly one month later, 1123A and route 677 will operate for the last time. (John Clarke)

1297 nears West India Docks; the 677 had to be extended beyond the limit of the tram service it replaced. The short stretch passed through dingy surroundings; this view says it all. (Denis Battams)

Approaching West India Docks terminus on 13th April 1959 is 1256 which has an inspector on board; the need for one at this backwater is open to question but it was a 'nice little number' to be positioned there. His presence prevents crews from arriving and leaving early.

POLICE OF THE
SCOTLAND YARD, S.W.I

65/Bus/2497(B.1.)

POSTAGE MUST BE PREPAID

GENERAL MANAGER
(OPERATION)
RECD 1 3 APR 1939

NEW SCOTLAND YARD
LONDON,
S.W.1

TELEPHONE · WHITEHALL 1212

/2ᵗʰ April, 1939.

Sir,

   With reference to your letter of the 15th February,
(DC/EB), I am directed by the Commissioner of Police of
the Metropolis to say that he considers that the traffic
conditions at the junction of West India Dock Road and
Commercial Road, will not permit the establishment of a
turning point for trolley vehicles there.

   In the circumstances, he regrets that he is unable
to agree to your proposal.

                    I am, Sir,

                         Your obedient Servant,

                              Secretary

1469.   WEST INDIA DOCK ROAD : TROLLEYBUS TURNING CIRCLE   1469.

   With reference to Minute No.3175 of the Vice-Chairman's Traffic Committee,
Mr. Buller submitted a memorandum dated 15th May reporting that at the
request of the Operating Manager, Trams & Trolleybuses, he had negotiated
with the London Midland & Scottish Railway Company for the acquisition of
part of their Goods Yard adjoining Ming Street for the establishment of a
trolleybus turning circle for the West India Dock service.   The price
originally asked by the Company for this land was £1,300 but they would be
prepared to accept £1,100 if they were allowed to retain a right-of-way
20 ft. wide adjacent to the Danish Church to give them additional access
to their Goods Yard.   The right-of-way was shown on the plan submitted.
The Board would also have to pay the cost of the necessary works.

   The Operating Manager, Trams & Trolleybuses, agreed to the second proposal
of the Company on the understanding that the right-of-way is used only as
a means of access to the Goods Yard and not as an exit, and that vehicles
enter the turning point at the same place as the trolleybuses and that they
do not stop whilst traversing the turning point.

   It was noted that if the right-of-way to the Goods Yard were allowed it
might interfere with the standing of trolleybuses on the turning circle
and was disadvantageous.   It was

        DECIDED: (a) that the Operating Manager, Trams & Trolleybuses,
                     decide whether or not the L.M. & S. Railway Company
                     be allowed the right-of-way across the turning circle
                     to the Goods Yard, and that the matter be concluded
                     as he directs; the matter to be judged from a traffic
                     point of view only;

                 (b) that a canteen be provided at the turning
                     circle and that a plan of the whole layout
                     of the turning circle, including the canteen,
                     be submitted to the Works Committee for approval.

1523.   WEST INDIA DOCK ROAD : TROLLEYBUS TURNING CIRCLE   1523.

   Mr. Buller submitted a memorandum dated 10th August reporting that
negotiations had taken place with the Poplar Borough Council for the
carrying out of certain works to facilitate the operation of the
proposed trolleybus turning circle at West India Dock Road terminus.
It was proposed that after the Board had acquired the necessary land
for the turning circle from the London Midland & Scottish Railway
Company they should surrender to the Council the margins of land,
shown coloured pink on Drawing No. PW.12150, in exchange for which
the Council would pave the margins and carry out minor improvements
at the junction of Ming Street with West India Dock Road, as shown
on the drawing.   It was estimated that the cost of the works to be
carried out by the Council would amount to £245 as compared with a
pro rata value of £165 for the land to be surrendered by the Board.

   Authority was asked to conclude the negotiations in accordance with
the terms set out above.

        APPROVED.

A prime time to have used the lay-by wire would have been on Sunday 12th October 1958 when the Southern Counties Touring Society used 622 for a trip around east London. But No...... too much of a performance for staff; 1245 has had its poles pulled down to enable 622 to pass. (Fred Ivey)

1269 sits in the sun at West India Docks on 10th June 1951. The road to the left leads to Cubitt Town; public transport to that dreary area only occurred when route 277 was extended beyond the 677 terminus of Ming Street – even then the full service did not reach Cubitt Town. Note the odd shaped bus stop flag fitted to a traction standard. (Clarence Carter)

Motorbuses occupy the stand now apart from Monday to Friday peak hour journeys to and from Commercial Road routes. RTL 1098 on the 277 is regularly seen here. 1643 creeps onto the stand almost shamefully; it is allocated to West Ham depot whose blind display for this location is amplified with a via point. (Fred Ivey)

When 677s got out of turn at West India Docks, one would normally drop its poles to allow the other to pass, however when one vehicle needed to jump two then the lay-by wire was likely to be used. 1248 and another 677 are on the stand; 1294 has its poles placed on the lay-by wire and will soon be off to Smithfield.

The Commercial Road trolleybus services served West India Docks; working on route 567 is L3 1488 – this is an evening summer-time view. Its next trip will be to Smithfield though it is unlikely that any passengers will make the full journey. Note the dock cranes in the background. (Don Thompson)

1145 approaches the un-salubrious terminus while 1262 is ready for its next trip to Balls Pond Road. It is Saturday 11th April 1959 and a new bus stop post is in position ready for bus route 277 which will start in four days' time; the original flag will not fit onto the new post and a more modern example will be provided – see photo of 1643 on page 149. (Jack Gready)

LIMEHOUSE TO GARDINERS CORNER

The 677 has been withdrawn and Limehouse junction is now only used by the Commercial Road routes. The facing and trailing frogs are for journeys to West India Docks. The photographer took this view on 17th October 1959. (John Gillham)

It is thought that the link from Commercial Road into West India Dock Road was installed from the beginning of trolleybus operation here (September 1939) though the first reference to these journeys appears in an Inspector's Timetable for 29th July 1942 which states that a Monday to Saturday morning peak hour service operated. A Monday to Friday evening peak hour service commenced on 13th April 1949. Over the years, routes 565/567/569/665 all had trips from 'London' termini to West India Docks. 1486 passes from Commercial Road into West India Dock Road on route 567. (Fred Ivey)

L3 1478 passes through the Limehouse complex on its way to Aldgate on route 567. Some journeys on this route turned right here for West India Docks. (Don Thompson)

1431 is about to pass through Limehouse trailing frog on 31st October 1959 (this is where East India Dock Road meets West India Dock Road). At Poplar from new, 1431 will be involved in stage four of the conversion programme but will stay locally for another six months as it will move to West Ham in eleven days' time. To Highgate at stage six and Fulwell at nine, 1431 was FW5 on 8th May 1962, the running number of the last trolleybus due into the depot that night. 1521 took up FW5 at Hampton Court at 10.45pm and became the last trolleybus to operate on the streets of London. 1431 ran in front carrying those who were unable to board 1521. (John Clarke)

A number of redundant tram bodies were used for various purposes. This is E1 1622 at Hayling Island and shows the notice concerning the replacement of tram route 65 by trolleybus services 565 and 665 on and after June 9th 1940. This tram was recovered and then restored to full operating condition and works at the National Tramway Museum at Crich. (Norman Rayfield)

The British Sailors Society was formed on 18th March 1818, providing pastoral care for seafarers. Passing by on 6th July 1959 while working on route 567 to Aldgate is L3 1481. (Peter Mitchell)

On 6th July 1959, L3 1501 passes under Stepney East railway bridge; the station is on the line to Fenchurch Street. Many trolley-buses advertised the London to Paris air race at this time with the Daily Mail giving the event full coverage. 1501 heads west for Clerkenwell Green on the 665. (Peter Mitchell)

Fog is clearing as 1481, heading for Barking, passes beneath the railway bridge at Stepney East during the late morning of 31st October 1959. Route 665 is one of three trolleybus routes using Commercial Road; there were also a number of bus routes along this main artery. (John Clarke)

The East End of London is by no means all gloomy as exemplified by 1479 seen in bright sunlight. Having just started from a set of traffic lights, 1479 is about to cross White Horse Road – about half way between Arbour Square and Stepney East. The feeder in the background was supplied from Stepney sub-station; there was emergency provision within the feeder pillar to switch to a feed from the one at Limehouse.

1510 is approaching Albert Gardens while working on route 567 to Aldgate on 24th January 1959. It is 3.52pm so daylight will soon fade. Two RTWs on route 15 can also be seen. (John Clarke)

The short-working facility at Arbour Square was a very useful turn-back in the later years of trolleybus operation. Routes 567/569/665 were subject to heavy delays and inspectors would have no hesitation in turning vehicles there so that they could regain their timing. As with many other short-working points, a facing frog, crossover and trailing frog are provided. This view was taken on 17th October 1959. (John Gillham)

For an unknown reason in later years most of the Sunday trips from Poplar to Aldgate (run specifically for Petticoat Lane market) ran instead from Canning Town to Arbour Square; this seemed pointless as the traffic objective of the market was lost. Maybe it is on one of these journeys that 1440 turns into Arbour Square. (Fred Ivey)

Poplar's 1431 is by the Arbour Square open space and under a bowstring bracket arm on the south side of the square. This vehicle was the penultimate trolleybus to operate in London. (Fred Ivey)

Having been curtailed at Arbour Square L3 1484 turns into East Arbour Square; its next trip is to Barking. Sent to Finchley at stage four of the conversion programme, it was surprisingly transferred to Stonebridge at stage twelve; a defect saw it taken out of service on 28th December 1961, a few days short of its planned withdrawal date. The fault did not make it unroadworthy as it travelled to Colindale depot under its own power for storage on 2nd January 1962. (Fred Ivey)

Arbour Square was situated in the centre of two adjacent roads – West Arbour Square and East Arbour Square. Standing in East Arbour Square on 1st November 1959 is 1442. (Norman Rayfield)

1487 leaves East Arbour Square at 3.55pm on 24th January 1959 – it has been curtailed due to late running. About to pass through the trailing frog is 1503 which heads east. (John Clarke)

1471 is at Dean Cross Street on 6th July 1959 working to Aldgate; the RTL on route 40 makes an attempt to overtake 1471 but it is unlikely that this will occur as trolleybuses are quicker. Although the ordinary man in the street might know whether a vehicle on the 567 was allocated to West Ham or Poplar by its depot code plate, he would be unable to do this with 1471 due to the absence of one. 1471 was one of the few L3s that had sliding window ventilators rather than half-drop windows. (Peter Mitchell)

1462 is at Berner Street and heading for Aldgate on route 567 at 2.04pm on 6th July 1959. Although the Poplar crews know that conversion to motorbuses takes place in about four months' time, those living in the locality probably have little or no knowledge about the impending change. (Peter Mitchell)

On one of Mr Dryhurst's rainy London trolleybus excursions 1435, with another L3 behind, waits at the traffic lights at Goodman's Stile (off to the right). Opposite is White Church Lane. While Aldgate trolleybus station was being resurfaced, White Church Lane was used as a temporary terminus for the Commercial Road/Whitechapel Road trolleybuses; this commenced in November 1954 but it is not known how long this situation lasted. (Michael Dryhurst)

Just east of Gardiners Corner Poplar's 1445 is another vehicle only working as far as Clerkenwell Green; they only worked that far west because the 555 paralleled it from there to Bloomsbury and there was insufficient trade for both routes to have a full service between the two points. The firm J.J. & S.W. Chalk are no more – the premises is now occupied by Premier Laser Clinic. (Brian Speller)

This is the stop prior to Gardiners Corner; on 27th July 1940, L3 1437 is in pristine condition and full wartime garb. The barber's SHAVING sign encourages men to enter. Trams have gone for only a number of weeks and a redundant crossover is seen in the foreground. Note the chains between posts on the pavement; this prevents people running into the roadway and getting run down. (Alan Cross)

| Running Number | | Ex. Depot | Barking New London Road | Wellington Road | East Ham Town Hall | Claughton Road | Green Street | Greengate | Bull Road | North Woolwich | Silvertown Station | Canning Town | Benledi Street | Aberfeldy Street | West India Docks | Gardiners Corner | Aldgate | Smithfield | Holborn | Bloomsbury | Forms | | | |
Poplar	West Ham																				Aldgate	Smithfield	Holborn	Blooms-
70				7.15			7.20	7.23				7.28		7.31		7.46	7.59					8.1		
73			7.11		7.17		21	24				29		32		47	7.50				7.52			
	8														7.34	47	50				52			
35				17			22	25				30		33		48		8.8					8.8	
48				14	20		24	27				32		35		50		8.10						8
	9			15	21		25	28				33		36		51	54			56				
34							7.16					33		36		51	54			59				
87										7.21		33		36		51	54			56				
78				15	21		25	28				33		36		51	8.4						8.6	
36				21			26	29				34		37		52		12			12			
116			17		23		27	30				35		38		53	56			59				
	22		19		25		29	32				37		40		55	58			8.2				
37				25			30	33				38		41		56		16					16	
74										22		39		42		57	8.0				3			
	20		21		27		31	34				39		42		57			17		2			
	25														44	57	0				2			
50			22		28		32	35				40		43		58			18					
45						7.32		35				40		43		58		11			13			
	3			29			34	37				42		45		8.0		20					20	
48			25		31		35	38				43		46		1	4				10			
88										27		44		47		2	5				7			
58			26		32		36	39				44		47		2			22					
92										33		45		48		3	6				8			
38			27		33		37	40				45		48		3		16					18	
67			28		34		38	41				46		49		4	7				10			
40				33			38	41				46		49		4		24					24	
77			29		35		39	42				47		50		5	8				11			
52			30		36		40	43				48		51		6			26					2
	5														54	7	10				13			
	1		31		37		41	44				49		52		7	10				15			
39										32		49		52		7	10				16			
42				37			42	45				50		53		8		28					28	
55			33		39		43	46				51		54		9		29						3
	18			39			44	47				52		55		10	23						25	
46			35		44		45	48				53		56		11	14				20			
81				41			46	49				54		57		12		32					32	
94										39		56		59		14	17				23			
83			38		44		48	51				56		59		14	17				23			
107										45		57		8.0		15	18				20			
51			39		45		49	52				57		0		15	28					30		
	17		40		46		50	53				58		1		16			36					3
41					45		50	53				58		1		16		36					36	
95			41		47		51	54				59		2		17	20				25			

trolleybuses)   (5,000, 3/42)

Running Number Poplar	West Ham	Ex. Depot (Poplar)	Bloomsbury	Holborn	Smithfield	Aldgate	Gardiners Corner	West India Docks	Aberfeldy Street	Benledi Street	Canning Town	Silvertown Station	North Woolwich	West Ham Depot	Greengate	Green Street	Claughton Road	East Ham Town Hall	Wellington Road	Barking New London Road	North Woolwich	Claughton Rd / Silvertown Station / Wellington Road (Forms)	Barking	West India Docks
18														7/25		7.31		7.37				7.39		
81						7 4	7 7		7 22		7.25				7.30	33		39				41		
96						5	8		23		26		7.43							7.45				
110		7/20							23		26				31	34	7.38	7.42					7.45	
59					6.56		9		24		27				32	35	39	43					46	
89					58		11		26		29				34	37	41	45					48	
41		7/23							26		29				34	37		43				45		
107						8	11		26		29	7.41							7.45					
	16		6.54				12		27		30				35	38	42	46					50	
	7					10	13		28		31				36	39	43	47					51	
49				7.1			14		29		32				37	40	44	48					53	
98						11	14		29		32		49					51						
	8					12	15	7 28																734
	6		7	7 1			17		32		35				40	43	47	51					54	
61			7 0				18		33		36				41	44	48	52					56	
80						16	19		34		37				42	45	49	53					59	
54					7		20		35		38				43	48/58								
100						17	20		35		38		55					59						
53			4				22		37		40				45	48	52	56					8 1	
114						20	23		38		41	53							57					
91				8			24		39		42				47	50		56				8.3		
	15					22	25		40		43				48	51	55	59					6	
	25					22	25	38																114
	21			13			26		41		44				49	52	56	8 0					5	
90			8				26		41		44				49	52	56	0					9	
101						23	26		41		44	8 1						8 7					11	
	10					24	27		42		45				50	53	57	1					11	
93				12			28		43		46				51	54	8 0						8	
84			12				30		45		48				53	56	8 0	4					14	
4				19			32		47		50				55	58		4					12	
2			16				32		47		50				55	58		4					13	
103						29	32		47		50	7						15						
66						30	33		48		51				56	59	3	7					16	
119			16				34		49		52				57	8 0	4	8					17	
	5					31	34	47																54
62						32	35		50		53	8 5							8 9					
64			7 20				36		51		54				59	2		8					18	
	19					34	37		52		55		8 0			3	7	11					21	
69			20				38		53		56				1	4	8	12					20	
63				26			39		54		57				2	5	9	13					19	
97			24				40		55		58				3	6		12				20		
86						38	41		56		59	16						16			8 22			
	11		24				42		57		8 0				5	8	12	16					24	

1654 and 1431 have arrived at Gardiners Corner together; 1654 will head down Commercial Street for Smithfield while 1431 will turn left for Aldgate. Rubbing shoulders here, both could be seen together at North Finchley between November 1959 and January 1961. They also could be seen side by side at Hammersmith between February 1961 and January 1962. Transfer movements for 1431: PR/HT 11.11.59. HT/FW 1.2.61. Transfer movement for 1654: WH/SE 11.11.59. (Fred Ivey)

West Ham's 1560 is on loan to Poplar. It was quite common for West Ham to loan trolleybuses to them but as PR only worked on the Barking Road/Commercial Road routes, the WH blinds (which incorporated 567 and 665) could have been left in. (Fred Ivey)

The Barking Road/Commercial Road trolleybus services were the most complex in London with vehicles moving from one route to another in the course of a day's work. L3 1515 displays '569 BARKING'; it is still on route 569 but the driver has already changed his blind for the next trip from Aldgate which is on the 567 to Barking. (Pamlin Prints)

The overhead complex is still complete when this view was taken on 18th July 1959; looking east a 567 already has its front blind changed for its next trip to Barking. Gardiners Corner took its name from the 'Gardiners' store at the junction of Commercial Road with Whitechapel Road. (John Gillham)

1439 traverses Gardiners Corner while working on the 567 to TRINITY CHURCH; four crossovers in quick succession have to be negotiated. In Commercial Street 1211 on the 647 heads for London Docks (its blind already changed for a return trip to Stamford Hill); 1666 on the 665 is alongside and without a front bullseye; maybe a replacement panel has been fitted and a transfer is yet to be applied. (Fred Ivey)

At Gardiners Corner on 31st October 1959, L3 1483 moves from Commercial Road into Commercial Street to link up with 647s from Leman Street. As with all trolleybus services here, drivers needed considerable skill to get through without getting caught on a dead section of overhead. Few, if any of those on board 1483 will be going to Smithfield – only about fifty passengers a day used this facility. (John Clarke)

GARDINERS CORNER TO LONDON DOCKS

A slender connection between the north and the east of the system was at Gardiners Corner. One route involved was the 647 on which service 1209 is seen. It is running late and has been curtailed at Stoke Newington on its northbound trip; 647s only occasionally turned at this location. (Tony Belton)

There is no excuse for the excessive 'blind slip' on 1136 (most of '643' is shown); latterly, winding gear mechanism became worn but respective crews have not looked to see if 647 is displayed. 1136 has passed a number of inspectors; maybe they were in shop doorways so only noticed the running number! Aldgate East station had two corner entrances; one is here at the top of Leman Street at its junction with Whitechapel High Street. There are black and white sleeves on traction poles that have traffic lights fixed to them; upon abandonment of trolleybuses in London, local authorities had to make new arrangements. (Tony Belton)

1326 on the 647 has arrived at Aldgate East and is working the last ever trip to DOWNHAM RD KINGSLAND ROAD; this occurred on Tuesday 18th July 1961, the date of stage eleven of the trolleybus conversion programme. Since the withdrawal of route 653 after operations on 31st January that year, the 647 was the only route to operate through this once very heavily used junction. (Don Lewis)

A bomb has fallen in the proximity of Gardiners Corner on 19th September 1940; the blast damage is very apparent in this view taken at the top of Leman Street. K1 1122 is only eighteen months old and although the damage may only appear superficial, that was not so as it cost £112 to repair the vehicle – in today's figures that is roughly £6000 (it has to be assumed that the frame and bodywork required a lot of work before it could be returned to service). Amazingly both of 1122's poles have stayed on the overhead – doubtless though, the power has been knocked off by the explosion. 1122 will be towed back to Stamford Hill depot for initial inspection before being sent to either Charlton or Fulwell Works for repair. In the foreground, conduit tram tracks can be seen – soon they will be lifted and be used in conjunction with the war effort.

It was just a short run from Gardiners Corner to London Docks; the only place of note was where two bridges carried the railway from Fenchurch Street to Shoeburyness, Southend and Tilbury. 1206 has just passed under the second of the bridges on its way to Stamford Hill. On the traction pole on the right, a poster details the replacement of route 647 by bus route 67 on 19th July 1961; these were pasted onto traction poles a few days before each conversion day. In the background is the wall of London Docks. (Tony Belton)

Looking in the opposite direction, 1205 is a couple of minutes away from London Docks terminus. Passing over the bridge is a British Railways former LMS 2.6.4 Tank heading into Fenchurch Street. It is 27th June 1959 – by this time two stages of the trolleybus conversion scheme have been implemented. (Jack Gready)

There was plenty of rain on the last Sunday of operation of the 647 (16th July 1961); it has dampened the spirits of motorists and pedestrians as evidenced by the lack of activity at Leman Street bridges; troughing is not only in position under the bridges but also between them. Cohen's were not allowed to remove wiring under bridges so in a few days' time London Transport staff will tie the redundant overhead off to adjacent traction standards. 1218 is followed by another 647. Cable Street is to the right. (Tony Belton)

Looking north and south at London Docks, 1335 and 1218 await their next trips to Stamford Hill on route 647. Both have the same permutation of linen/paper blinds – 1218 is another 647 with a badly set route blind. There were no refreshment facilities here and crews had to wait until they got to Stamford Hill before they could down a cup of tea. (Don Lewis)

The London Docks terminus of route 647 was at the bottom of Dock Street and in uninspiring surroundings. 1130 was always at Stamford Hill depot, but is now nearing the end of its life. (Peter Moore)

1206 is in East Smithfield as it moves around the circle at the bottom of Dock Street. The TROLLEY BUSES TURNING notice invites other road users to take caution; this notice was only positioned here in the second half of the 1950s – maybe an incident prompted its use. (Chris Orchard)

Although it might have appeared to have been a tight turn at the bottom of Dock Street, drivers made it with ease as long as they had the trolleybus on full lock at the commencement of the turn. This is demonstrated by 1108 as it completes the manoeuvre at London Docks. (Peter Moore)

The last trolleybus to leave London Docks was 1135 on route 647. It is seen on arrival and waits time on Tuesday 18th July 1961; when it speeds away, a trolleybus will never be seen in the vicinity of London's docklands again. Though it is 'final ever departure', the driver shows the correct display for Stamford Hill depot – even though the last passengers will alight in Stamford Hill itself. Who 'chalked up' 1135? – take a guess! Chalk obtained from Orange Hill Grammar School for boys. (Terry Cooper)